THE BILINGUAL SERIES OF
THE MOST IMPRESSIVE BEAUTY OF CHINA

最美中国双语系列

杰出人物

HALL OF FAME

主　编◎青　闻
副主编◎成正凯　王艳玲
参　编◎成研言　宋　娟　曹　阳

中国科学技术大学出版社

内容简介

"最美中国双语系列"是一套精品文化推广图书,包括《风景名胜》《民俗文化》《饮食文化》《杰出人物》《科技成就》《中国故事》六册,旨在传播中华优秀文化,传承中华民族宝贵的民族精神,展示奋进中的最美中国,可供广大中华文化爱好者、英语学习者及外国友人参考使用。

本书介绍了中华民族部分代表性的杰出人物,包括圣贤先哲、领袖人物、社稷名流、科技英才、文史巨匠、艺术大师、体坛名人等。

图书在版编目(CIP)数据

杰出人物:英汉对照/青闰主编.—合肥:中国科学技术大学出版社,2021.11

(最美中国双语系列)

ISBN 978-7-312-05230-9

Ⅰ.杰… Ⅱ.青… Ⅲ.名人—生平事迹—中国—英、汉 Ⅳ.K825.46

中国版本图书馆CIP数据核字(2021)第121015号

杰出人物
JIECHU RENWU

出版	中国科学技术大学出版社 安徽省合肥市金寨路96号,230026 http://press.ustc.edu.cn https://zgkxjsdxcbs.tmall.com
印刷	合肥市宏基印刷有限公司
发行	中国科学技术大学出版社
经销	全国新华书店
开本	880 mm×1230 mm 1/32
印张	9.375
字数	226千
版次	2021年11月第1版
印次	2021年11月第1次印刷
定价	35.00元

前 言 Preface

　　文化是一个国家与民族的灵魂。"最美中国双语系列"旨在弘扬和推广中华优秀文化，突出文化鲜活主题，彰显文化核心理念，挖掘文化内在元素，拓展文化宽广视野，为广大读者了解、体验和传播中华文化精髓提供全新的视角。本系列图书秉持全面、凝练、准确、实用、自然、流畅的撰写原则，全方位、多层面、多角度地展现中华文化的源远流长和博大精深，对于全民文化素质的提升具有独特的现实意义，同时也为世界文化的互联互通提供必要的借鉴和可靠的参考。

　　"最美中国双语系列"包括《风景名胜》《民俗文化》《饮食文化》《杰出人物》《科技成就》《中国故事》六册，每册中的各篇文章以文化剪影以主线，以佳句点睛、情景对话和生词注解为副线，别出心裁，精彩呈现中华文化的方方面面。

　　"最美中国双语系列"充分体现以读者为中心的编写理念，从文化剪影到生词注解，读者可由简及繁、由繁及精、由精及思地感知中华文化的独特魅力。书中的主线和副线是一体两面的有机结合，不可分割，如果说主线是灵魂，副线则是灵魂的眼睛。

　　"最美中国双语系列"的推出，是讲好中国故事、展现中国立场、传播中国文化的一道盛宴，读者可以从中感悟生活。

　　《杰出人物》包括圣贤先哲、领袖人物、社稷名流、科技英才、文史巨匠、艺术大师和体坛名人七部分，这里有睿智旷达的老子、孔子、孙

杰出人物

子、孟子、庄子,有雄才大略的秦始皇、汉武帝、隋文帝、唐太宗、成吉思汗、康熙,有博古通今的李冰、蔡伦、张衡、祖冲之、沈括、李时珍,有一心为国的华罗庚、钱学森、邓稼先,有文采斐然的李白、杜甫、李商隐、鲁迅、巴金、金庸,还有挥洒自如的王羲之、顾恺之、吴道子、齐白石、徐悲鸿,更有力挫群雄的姚明、李娜……可谓群星璀璨,熠熠生辉。

　　本书由焦作大学成正凯和新疆师范大学成研言撰写初稿,焦作大学王艳玲撰写二稿,人民邮电出版社宋娟、焦作师范专科学校曹阳撰写三稿,焦作大学青闰负责全书统稿与定稿。

　　最后,在本书即将付梓之际,衷心感谢中国科学技术大学出版社的大力支持,感谢朋友们的一路陪伴,感谢家人们始终不渝的鼓励和支持。

青　闰

2021年3月6日

目 录 Contents

前言　Preface ………………………………………………………… i

第一部分　圣贤先哲
Part Ⅰ　Sages and Philosophers

老子　Lao Tzu …………………………………………………… 003
孔子　Confucius ………………………………………………… 009
孟子　Mencius …………………………………………………… 015
庄子　Zhuang Tzu ……………………………………………… 021
孙子　Sun Tzu …………………………………………………… 027

第二部分　领袖人物
Part Ⅱ　Leading Figures

秦始皇　The First Emperor of Qin ………………………… 035
汉武帝　Emperor Wu of Han ………………………………… 041
隋文帝　Emperor Wen of Sui ………………………………… 047
唐太宗　Emperor Taizong of Tang ………………………… 053
成吉思汗　Genghis Khan ……………………………………… 059
康熙皇帝　Emperor Kangxi …………………………………… 065

第三部分 社稷名流
Part Ⅲ Distinguished Personages

张骞　Zhang Qian ·· 075

玄奘　Xuanzang ·· 081

郑和　Zheng He ·· 087

郑成功　Zheng Chenggong ·· 094

林则徐　Lin Zexu ·· 100

第四部分 科技英才
Part Ⅳ Scientific Geniuses

蔡伦　Cai Lun ·· 109

李时珍　Li Shizhen ·· 115

钱学森　Qian Xuesen ·· 122

邓稼先　Deng Jiaxian ·· 129

华罗庚　Hua Luogeng ·· 136

屠呦呦　Tu Youyou ·· 142

第五部分 文史巨匠
Part Ⅴ Great Masters of Literature and History

屈原　Qu Yuan ·· 151

目 录

司马迁　Sima Qian ·· 157

李白　Li Bai ·· 163

杜甫　Du Fu ·· 169

李商隐　Li Shangyin ·· 175

苏轼　Su Shi ·· 181

吴承恩　Wu Cheng'en ······································ 187

曹雪芹　Cao Xueqin ·· 193

鲁迅　Lu Xun ··· 199

巴金　Ba Jin ··· 205

金庸　Louis Cha ·· 211

第六部分　艺术大师
Part VI Great Masters of Art

王羲之　Wang Xizhi ·· 221

顾恺之　Gu Kaizhi ·· 227

吴道子　Wu Daozi ··· 234

齐白石　Qi Baishi ·· 241

徐悲鸿　Xu Beihong ·· 247

张大千　Chang Dai-Chien ·································· 254

梅兰芳　Mei Lanfang ······································· 261

李小龙　Bruce Lee ··· 268

杰出人物

第七部分 体坛名人
Part VII Sports Celebrities

姚明　Yao Ming ……………………………………………277
李娜　Li Na ……………………………………………284

第一部分　圣贤先哲

Part Ⅰ　Sages and Philosophers

老子

Lao Tzu

导入语 Lead-in

老子(约前571~前471?),姓李名耳,字聃,一字伯阳,春秋末期楚国人。中国古代思想家、哲学家、文学家和史学家,道家学说创始人,被尊称为"道家始祖"。老子在函谷关前所著《道德经》,上篇为《道经》,下篇为《德经》,道是德之"体",德乃道之"用"。《道德经》《易经》和《论语》被认为是对中国人影响最深远的三部思想巨著。老子思想的核心是朴素辩证法,主张无为而治、以柔克刚、物极必反、道法自然。老子的哲学思想和他创立的道家学派,对中国两千多年来思想文化的发展产生了深远的影响。德国哲学家黑格尔、尼采,俄罗斯作家托尔斯泰等都有关于《道德经》的专著或专论。

20世纪80年代,根据联合国教科文组织统计,在被译成外文并出版的世界文化名著中,发行量最大的是《圣经》,其次就是《道德经》。老子的著作和思想早已成为世界历史文化遗产中弥足珍贵的精神财富。

文化剪影　Cultural Outline

　　The Book of Tao and Teh, also called *Lao Tzu,* can be divided into two parts—*Tao* (*Dao*) and *Teh* (*De*)—with eighty-one chapters. **Revered**① as a classic by Chinese Taoists, it is not only one of the fundamental texts of Chinese thought, but also has been highly **acknowledged**② as one of the enlightening books in world literature.

　　《道德经》一书,又称《老子》,全书分《道经》和《德经》两部分,共计81章。作为中国道家经典,它不仅是中国思想的基础文本之一,而且被公认为世界文学作品中颇具启发性的著作之一。

　　Lao Tzu is full of wisdom and has a keen eye for observing things. His representative work entitled *The Book of Tao and Teh* is the first complete **philosophical**③ work in China, which has sublime words with deep meaning, covering the great wisdom of life. Because *The Book of Tao and Teh* is widely circulated and accepted by Taoism, Lao Tzu's image has been elevated to the status of deity and has become the **incarnation**④ of "Tao".

　　老子思想睿智,观察事物目光敏锐。其代表作《道德经》是中国首部完整的哲学著作，思想内容微言大义，涵盖了人生大智慧。由于《道德经》广为流传，并被道教接受，因此老子的形象被提升到了神圣的地位，成为"道"的化身。

The Book of Tao and Teh summarizes the main tenets of Taoism, which is a kind of philosophy and religion, whose dominant image is "Tao", and which enables individuals to achieve harmony and a more profound level of understanding of life. Under the influence of various new thoughts of Taoism in the new historical period, Lao Tzu's thought became more **intricate**⑤ and his status in culture was improved **correspondingly**⑥.

《道德经》概括了道家的主要教义，道家是一种哲学和宗教，其主导形象是"道"，它能使人身心和谐并对生活产生更深刻的理解。在新时期各种道学新思潮的影响下，老子的思想变得更加复杂，其在文化中的地位也得到相应提高。

佳句点睛　Punchlines

1. The Book of Tao and Teh written by Lao Tzu is one of the popular works in Chinese classical literature.

老子所著的《道德经》是中国古典文学中颇受欢迎的作品之一。

2. The Book of Tao and Teh, The Book of Changes and The Analects of Confucius are considered to be the three greatest **ideological**⑦

works that have had the most profound influence on the Chinese people.

《道德经》《易经》和《论语》被认为是对中国人影响最深远的三部思想巨著。

3. Lao Tzu put forward profound and thorough questions and looked at them from a different **perspective**⑧.

老子提出了深刻而透彻的问题,并从不同的角度看待它们。

 情景对话　Situational Dialogue

A: How do you feel about reading books for a college student?

B: It can help me explore the nature of human beings and gives spiritual and psychological relief.

A: Great. Why should young people read Chinese classics?

B: We all know that classics are a kind of treasure in a nation. Reading the classics is beneficial to the character development and personal growth of the young people, it also provides a chance for them to enhance their aesthetic taste as most of classics has a very unique language style.

A: Who impresses you most about Chinese classics?

B: Lao Tzu.

A: Oh, why?

B: Because I'm impressed by the philosophy of Lao Tzu, whose words are all wise sayings, such as "Overcoming hardness with softness" "The highest good is like water" "A journey of a thousand miles starts with the first step" "Good fortune follows upon disaster; disaster **lurks**① within good fortune", and so on, which provide a **guideline**② for the development of human society in future.

A: Thank you. It is better to listen to your words than to read for ten years.

B: That's nothing. I'm flattered.

A: 作为大学生,你对阅读的感受如何?

B: 阅读可以帮助我探索人类的本质,给予我精神上和心理上的慰藉。

A: 好极了,为什么年轻人应该读经典名著?

B: 我们都知道,经典名著是一个民族的财富。阅读经典名著有利于青少年性格的培养和个人的成长,也为他们提供了一个提高审美情趣的机会,因为大多数经典名著都有非常独特的语言风格。

A: 你对中国古典文学印象最深的作者是谁?

B: 老子。

A: 为什么?

B: 因为老子的哲学给我留下了深刻印象,他说的话都是至理名言,比如"柔弱胜刚强""上善若水""千里之行,始于足下""祸兮,福之所倚;福兮,祸之所伏"等,为我们人类社会未来的发展指明了方向。

A: 谢谢你。听君一席话,胜读十年书。

B: 哪里哪里。你过奖了。

生词注解 Notes

① revere /rɪˈvɪə(r)/ *vt.* 崇敬；尊敬

② acknowledged /əkˈnɒlɪdʒd/ *adj.* 公认的；确定收到的

③ philosophical /ˌfɪləˈsɒfɪkl/ *adj.* 哲学的；哲理的

④ incarnation /ˌɪnkɑːˈneɪʃn/ *n.* 化身；典型体现

⑤ intricate /ˈɪntrɪkət/ *adj.* 复杂的；错综的

⑥ correspondingly /ˌkɒrəˈspɒndɪŋli/ *adv.* 相应地；一致地

⑦ ideological /ˌaɪdiəˈlɒdʒɪkl/ *adj.* 思想的；意识形态的

⑧ perspective /pəˈspektɪv/ *n.* 视角；观点

⑨ lurk /lɜːk/ *vi.* 潜伏；埋伏

⑩ guideline /ˈɡaɪdlaɪn/ *n.* 指导方针；指导原则

孔子

Confucius

 导入语 Lead-in

孔子(前551~前479),本名孔丘,字仲尼,生于山东曲阜,春秋末期鲁国人。中国古代伟大的思想家、教育家、政治家和儒学创始人。孔子开启私学教育,一生倡导仁、义、礼、智、信。政治上,他主张为政以德,齐之以礼,即用"德"来约束人民,用"礼"来教化人民;教育上,他主张因材施教,注重学生的个性教育,他弟子众多,如子贡、子路、颜回等。孔子的言行思想被弟子整理为《论语》,因其国内外影响深远而被列为世界十大文化名人之首。爱默生认为"孔子是全世界各民族的光荣"。

 文化剪影　Cultural Outline

Confucius, with high **aspirations**① and great ambitions as a boy, was keen on reading and learning. He travalled thousands of miles to study rites from Lao Tzu in Luoyi. He had been an official of the Lu state, but his thought seemed to have fallen on deaf ears. Thus, he devoted himself to education and became the first to start private education in Chinese educational history. It is said that he had three thousand disciples, among whom there were seventy-two **prominent**② ones. He, together with his disciples, took a painstaking tour to give lectures among the states of the time. In late years, he compiled *Poetry*, *History*, *Rites* and *Music*, made notes on *The Book of Changes*, and revised *Spring and Autumn Annals* in late years; they were commonly described as "The Six Classics".

孔子自幼志向远大，热衷学习。他千里奔波至洛邑向老子学习礼法。孔子曾做过鲁国的官员，但其思想并未被人采纳。于是，他投身教育，成为中国教育史上开办私学的第一人。据传孔子有弟子三千，贤者七十有二。他不辞辛劳，带领学生周游列国讲学。晚年，他编写《诗》《书》《礼》《乐》，注《易经》，修《春秋》，合称"六经"。

The Analects of Confucius was ranked as the first of "The Four Books", so Confucius was regarded as the founder of Confucianism. Many of his ideas, such as "Governing by Virtue" "The World for the

Common Good" "Guiding with Morality and **Regulating**③ with Rites," and so forth, are full of vitality till now. His core thought is nothing but "ren" (**benevolence**④)—the benevolent loves others, namely, to express filial piety to parents, love for the people and loyalty to the motherland. "Benevolence" implies the essence of traditional Chinese culture—the spirit of Harmony.

《论语》被列为儒家"四书"之首,所以孔子被视为儒家学说的创始人。他的很多主张如"为政以德""天下为公""道之以德,齐之以礼"等,至今依然富有生命力。孔子的核心思想莫过于"仁",仁者爱人,也就是,孝顺父母,热爱人民,忠诚祖国。"仁"隐含了中华传统文化的本质特征——和谐精神。

Confucius left behind countless famous educational sayings, inspiring a great number of students at home and abroad. For example, "I was not born wise" "In the company of three, there must be my teacher" "Fair Education for All" "Teach based on **aptitude**⑤" "Learn for practice," and so on, which have made Confucius one of the great teachers in the world.

孔子留下了无数教育名言,启发了国内外莘莘学子,如"我非生而知之者""三人行,必有我师焉""有教无类""因材施教""学以致用"等,这让孔子成为世界上伟大的老师之一。

佳句点睛　Punchlines

1. It can be a teacher to review the old and know the new.

温故而知新,可以为师矣。

2. To say you know when you know and to say you don't when you don't, that is true knowledge.

知之为知之,不知为不知,是知也。

3. Is it not happy to learn and practice? Is it not pleasing when there's a friend coming from afar? Is it not a gentleman that one isn't annoyed when others don't know of him?

学而时习之,不亦说乎? 有朋自远方来,不亦乐乎? 人不知而不愠,不亦君子乎?

情景对话　Situational Dialogue

A: Have you heard of Confucius, Alice?

B: Sure. He made a great influence on Chinese education and even world's culture. He deserves to be known as a great thinker.

A: He said, "Is it not pleasing when there's a friend coming from afar?" He also said, "We are all brothers upon the four seas." But generally, we Chinese people love him for his ideas in learning.

B: Sounds interesting. I'm all ears.

A: For example, "In the presence of a good man, think all the time how you may learn to equal him. In the presence of a bad man, turn your gaze within" "Choose those who are good and follow them, and those who are bad and change them" "He that would do well in his work must first sharpen his tools" "Learning without thought is labor lost; thought without learning is **perilous**⑥".

B: Is there anything else?

A: For example, "Haste makes waste" "Be **insatiable**⑦ in learning and tireless in teaching" "To Prefer it than to only know it. To delight in it is better than merely to prefer it".

B: Confucius really lived up to his reputation.

A: He had a lot of insights in other fields besides study, such as the way dealing with people, governance, and so on.

B: I'll calm down to study Confucius **conscientiously**⑧ and become a great scholar like him.

A: 爱丽丝,你听说过孔子吗?

B: 当然听说过。他对中国教育乃至世界文化都产生了重大的影响。他称得上是一位伟大的思想家。

A: 他说过:"有朋自远方来,不亦乐乎?"他还说:"四海之内皆兄弟也。"不过,我们中国人之所以崇敬他,是因为他的学习理念。

B: 这听起来很有意思。我愿意洗耳恭听。

A: 比如,"见贤思齐焉,见不贤而内自省也""择其善者而从之,其不善者而改之""工欲善其事,必先利其器""学而不思则罔,思而不学则殆"。

B:还有吗?

A:有啊,比如,"欲速则不达""学而不厌,诲人不倦""知之者不如好之者,好之者不如乐之者"。

B:孔子真是名不虚传啊!

A:除了学习方面,他在其他方面还有好多真知灼见呢,比如为人处世、治国理政等。

B:今后我一定要静下心来好好学习孔子的思想,做一名像他那样的大学问家。

生词注解　Notes

① aspiration /ˌæspəˈreɪʃn/　*n.* 愿望;抱负

② prominent /ˈprɒmɪnənt/　*adj.* 显著的;杰出的

③ regulate /ˈreɡjuleɪt/　*vt.* 调节;规定

④ benevolence /bəˈnevələns/　*n.* 仁慈;善行

⑤ aptitude /ˈæptɪtjuːd/　*n.* 天资;天赋

⑥ perilous /ˈperələs/　*adj.* 危险的;冒险的

⑦ insatiable /ɪnˈseɪʃəbl/　*adj.* 不知足的;贪得无厌的

⑧ conscientiously /ˌkɒnʃɪˈenʃəsli/　*adv.* 认真地;诚心诚意地

孟子

Mencius

 导入语　Lead-in

孟子(前372～前289)，原名孟轲，字子舆，战国时期邹国(今山东邹城北凫村)人，鲁国贵族孟孙氏的后裔。孟子是中国古代著名的思想家、教育家、政治家、哲学家和文学家，儒家思想重要代表人物之一，被后世尊称为"亚圣"。南宋朱熹将《孟子》与《论语》《大学》《中庸》合称为"四书"。《孟子》倡导"以仁为本"。孟子提出了"民为贵，社稷次之，君为轻"的主张，认为民心对于国家治乱兴亡至关重要。孟子的主要哲学思想是"性善论"，这也是他的核心思想体系。此外，孟子把道德规范概括为仁、义、礼、智，提出了"法先王"的道德准则，推崇尧舜之道。

文化剪影　Cultural Outline

In terms of humanity, Mencius believed that "human nature is **intrinsically**① good". He held that mankind is born with the four virtues such as Ren (benevolence), Yi (righteousness), Li (**propriety**②) and Zhi (wisdom) and that mankind can maintain and extend these through **introspection**③. In terms of politics, he believed in the **invincibility**④ of benevolent governance, strongly advocated implementing it and put forward the view that "people are more important than the ruler". In terms of philosophy, Mencius thought that the objective world has its own laws that cannot be violated, so that mankind should learn about the world and grasp its objective laws so as to change it. In terms of education, he **affirmed**⑤ the educational concept of "teaching the students in accordance with their aptitude" advanced by Confucius and further proposed that there must be certain standards in education so that students can have a definite goal to strive for.

在人性方面，孟子主张"性善论"，认为人生来就具备仁、义、礼、智四种品德，并认为人可以通过内省去保持和扩充这些美德；在政治方面，孟子主张仁政，提出了"民贵君轻"的观点，认为实行王道就可以无敌于天下；在哲学方面，孟子认为人不能违背客观世界的规律，因而人要认识世界，掌握客观规律，才能改造世界；在教育方面，孟子肯定了孔子提出的"因材施教"的教育理念，并进一步提出教育学生必须有一定的标准，使学生有一个明确的奋斗目标。

Mencius inherited and developed the Confucian theory, and upgraded the Confucian thought of "benevolent people loving others" to "benevolent governance", making the Confucian school a political school that cannot be ignored in the political circle of China. His people-centered thought was adopted by later rulers to **appease**⑥ the people and consolidate their rule. *Mencius* written by Mencius and his disciples ranks among "The Four Books" with achievements far beyond the "The Five Classics".

孟子继承和发展了儒家学说,将孔子"仁者爱人"的思想升华为"仁政"思想,使儒家学派成为中国政坛上一股不可忽视的力量;其民本思想被后来的统治者用于安抚人心、巩固统治;其与弟子所著的《孟子》位列"四书",成就远在"五经"之上。

Mencius believed that "one prospers in worries and hardships and perishes in ease and comfort", so only we think of danger in times of safety can we always be prepared for the worst. Meanwhile, he adhered to the principle that "neither riches nor honors can corrupt him; neither poverty nor lowly conditions can make him swerve from principles; neither threats nor force can bend him". Also, he proposed that "the people are the most important, next comes the country, and last the ruler".

孟子认为"生于忧患,死于安乐",只有居安思危,才能有备无患。同时,他坚持"富贵不能淫,贫贱不能移,威武不能屈"的做人原则。他还提出了"民为贵,社稷次之,君为轻"的主张。

杰出人物

佳句点睛 Punchlines

1. Mencius was a famous thinker, educator, statesman, philosopher and **litterateur**① in ancient China.

孟子是中国古代著名的思想家、教育家、政治家、哲学家和文学家。

2. Mencius is one of the most important representatives of **Confucianism**②, and was honored as "the Sage Next Best to Confucius" in later times. He, along with Confucius, was honored as "Confucius and Mencius".

孟子是儒家思想的重要代表人物之一,被后世尊称为"亚圣",与孔子合称"孔孟"。

3. Mencius inherited and developed the thoughts of Confucius, which have had a profound influence on Chinese culture of later generations.

孟子继承并发扬了孔子的思想,对后世的中国文化影响深远。

情景对话 Situational Dialogue

A: What book are you reading, Helen?
B: I'm reading a book about Mencius.

A: Really? What do you know about Mencius?

B: I know that Mencius was one of the most important representatives of Confucianism. He left us with many words of wisdom, for example, "Benevolence is **invincible**②" "A just cause has many supporters, while an unjust cause has few" "Nothing can be accomplished without norms and standards".

A: That's right. Have you heard of the story of *Three Removals of Mencius's Mother*?

B: That sounds interesting. Can you tell me the story?

A: No problem. After the death of his father, Mencius's mother raised him alone. In order to provide him with a good learning **environment**③, he and his mother moved three times, from the cemetery to the market, and then to the private school at last.

B: Mencius's mother was really good and considerate!

A: Sure. As an old saying goes, "If you keep company with dogs, you will become black." Perhaps it was because of the good learning environment that Mencius became a successful man.

A: 海伦,你在看什么书?

B: 我在看一本关于孟子的书。

A: 是吗?关于孟子你了解多少?

B: 我知道孟子是儒家思想的重要代表人物之一。他给我们留下了许多至理名言,比如"仁者无敌""得道多助,失道寡助""不以规矩,不成方圆"等。

A: 说得没错。那你听说过《孟母三迁》的故事吗？

B: 听起来很有趣,你能给我讲讲吗?

A: 没问题。孟子的父亲去世后,母亲独自抚养他。为了给孟子提供一个良好的学习环境,母亲带着他三次搬家,从墓地旁搬到集市边上,再到私塾附近。

B: 孟母真是一位用心良苦的好母亲。

A: 是啊。俗话说:"近朱者赤,近墨者黑。"也许正是因为有了良好的学习环境,孟子才能成才吧。

生词注解　Notes

① intrinsically /ɪnˈtrɪnsɪklɪ/　*adv.* 本质地;内在地

② propriety /prəˈpraɪətɪ/　*n.* 礼节;得体

③ introspection /ˌɪntrəˈspɛkʃən/　*n.* 内省;反省

④ invincibility /ɪnˌvɪnsəˈbɪlətɪ/　*n.* 无敌;不可战胜

⑤ affirm /əˈfɜːm/　*vt.* 肯定;断言

⑥ appease /əˈpiːz/　*vt.* 使……平息;使……和缓

⑦ litterateur /ˌlɪtərəˈtɜː/　*n.* 文学家;文人

⑧ Confucianism /kənˈfjuːʃənɪzəm/　*n.* 儒家思想

⑨ invincible /ɪnˈvɪnsəbl/　*adj.* 无敌的;不能征服的

⑩ environment /ɪnˈvaɪrənmənt/　*n.* 自然环境;生存环境

庄子

Zhuang Tzu

 **导入语　Lead-in**

庄子(约前369~前286),本名庄周,字子休,战国中期宋国人,楚庄王后裔,杰出的思想家、哲学家、文学家,庄子学派的创始人,道家学派的重要代表,他的学说与老子的学说并称为"老庄"。庄子继承了老子的道家学说,并多有超越,形成了自己独特而完备的思想体系。庄子学识渊博、崇尚自由、冷眼观世,主张"天人合一""清静无为"。庄子想象丰富、语言宏丽、挥洒自如、灵活多变、引人入胜。庄子的代表作有《逍遥游》《齐物论》等,他的作品被称为"文学的哲学,哲学的文学"。庄子及其学说不仅在中国古代

思想文化领域占有重要地位,而且促进了中国思想文化史的深远发展。

文化剪影 Cultural Outline

Zhuang Tzu is a collection of reasoning prose, which consists of three parts, in which there are inner chapters, outer chapters and **miscellaneous**① chapters. The inner part was written by Zhuang Tzu himself, whose rhetoric is like floating clouds and flowing water, subtle but profound in argument. The outer and miscellaneous parts were the interpretation of Zhuang Tzu's thought by others, including his disciples and other figures of Zhuang Tzu's school of thought, with vivid examples and lively expressions. *Zhuang Tzu* is described as "philosophy in literature and literature in philosophy".

《庄子》是一部说理散文集,分为内篇、外篇和杂篇:内篇为庄子自著,语言行云流水,说理幽微深邃;外篇和杂篇是他人(包括庄子门徒和其他庄子学派人物)对庄子思想的阐发,举例生动,语言活泼。《庄子》被喻为"文学的哲学,哲学的文学"。

Through the **explication**② of Zhuang Tzu's thought, *Zhuang Tzu* not only develops a unique school of thought in the Chinese philosophy, but also takes up an important position in the classic literature of China. His thought of "being a saint internally but a king externally" became an elementary proposition for Confucianism. Its **circuitous**③ narrative mode is consistent with the yin-yang theory, illustrating subtle philosophy with a fascinating language, which made it on a par with *The Book of Changes* and *The Book of Tao and Teh*. He took fables as a form of reasoning to create a style of romantic prose, which had a great influence on the shaping of personality and the creation style of numerous literati in history. Mr. Wen Yiduo commented that "there is always the imprint of Zhuang Tzu in the Chinese culture".

《庄子》通过对庄子思想的阐发,不仅在中国哲学领域独树一帜,而且在中国古典文学领域也占据重要地位。庄子提出的"内圣外王"思想成为儒家学说的基本命题。《庄子》合乎阴阳之道的曲折叙事模式,用引人入胜的语言阐释微妙难言的哲理,让其与《易经》和《道德经》相媲美。庄子把寓言作为一种说理形式,开创了浪漫主义风格的散文,对历史上众多文人的人格塑造和创作风格具有重大影响。闻一多先生评论说"中国人的文化里永远留着庄子的烙印"。

Zhuang Tzu had a fantastic imagination and a unique **perspective**[5] on everything in the world. His masterpiece *Zhuang Tzu* is the first work making use of fables as a literary form. Zhuang Tzu was good at adopting weird and **exaggerated**[6] images to symbolize and **allegorize**[7] the gist of thought, which was quite different from other thinkers of his time in literature and art. Mr. Lu Xun commented that "In the late Zhou Dynasty, the works of all schools could not surpass him".

庄子想象奇特,对世间万物有着独特的观察视角。其代表作《庄子》是首部把寓言作为文学形式运用的著作。庄子善于用诡异夸张的形象来象征、讽喻思想主旨，在文学艺术方面与同时期其他的思想家迥然不同。鲁迅先生评价说："晚周诸子之作，莫能先也。"

佳句点睛　Punchlines

1. A saint goes not for himself, an immortal not for merits and a sage not for fame.

至人无己，神人无功，圣人无名。

2. The friendship between the gentlemen is as light as water, while the communication between the mean people is as sweet as wine.

君子之交淡若水，小人之交甘若醴。

3. Like floating clouds and flowing water in rhetoric and subtle but profound in argumentation, *Zhuang Tzu* is described as "philosophy in literature and literature in philosophy".

《庄子》的语言如行云流水，说理幽微深邃，被喻为"文学的哲学，哲学的文学"。

情景对话　Situational Dialogue

A: Could you tell me what "Lao-Zhuang Philosophy" is, Mr. Chen?

B: It's a system of philosophy based on the ideas of both Lao Tzu and Zhuang Tzu.

A: Their names are put together in the term. Does it mean they are familiar with each other?

B: No. It just means they are similar in thought. They lived in different times. Zhuang Tzu inherited Lao Tzu's idea that "Tao follows nature" and developed Taoism into a real school of thought. Taoism was founded on the basis of Lao-Zhuang Philosophy.

A: There is a comment that "there is always the imprint of Zhuang Tzu in the Chinese culture". What do you think about it?

B: It came from Mr. Wen Yiduo, a famous **patriotic**① scholar. The imprint refers to Zhuang Tzu's great influence. His *Zhuang Tzu* built up a peculiar world of imagination, where there are extraordinary images and **capricious**② fables. His prose, boundless, imaginative and magnificent, is typical of romantic style, admired by countless later generations of scholars.

A: He is really a great scholar.

A：陈先生，请问什么是"老庄哲学"？
B：这是一种基于老子和庄子思想的哲学体系。
A：他们的名字并列在这个词语里，说明他们彼此熟悉吗？
B：不，这只是说他们思想类似。他们生活在不同的时代，庄子继承了老子"道法自然"的思想，把道家发展成了一种真正的思想流派。道家就是建立在"老庄哲学"之上的。

A: 有一句评论说:"中国人的文化里永远留着庄子的烙印。"你怎么看?

B: 这句话出自著名爱国学者闻一多先生。"烙印"体现了庄子的巨大影响。《庄子》一书营造了一个奇特的想象世界,其中的意象超乎寻常,语言变幻莫测。庄子的散文汪洋恣肆,想象丰富,气势磅礴,具有典型的浪漫主义风格,为无数后世文人所仰慕。

A: 他真是一位了不起的文人。

生词注解 Notes

① miscellaneous /ˌmɪsəˈleɪniəs/　*adj.* 混杂的;多种多样的

② circuitous /səˈkjuːɪtəs/　*adj.* 迂回的

③ perspective /pəˈspektɪv/　*n.* 观点;角度

④ explication /ˌeksplɪˈkeɪʃn/　*n.* 详细解释;说明

⑤ exaggerated /ɪɡˈzædʒəreɪtɪd/　*adj.* 夸张的;言过其实的

⑥ allegorize /ˈæləɡəraɪz/　*v.* 讽喻化;使……寓言化

⑦ patriotic /ˌpætriˈɒtɪk/　*adj.* 爱国的;有爱国心的

⑧ capricious /kəˈprɪʃəs/　*adj.* 变幻莫测的;反复无常的

圣贤先哲 第一部分

孙子

Sun Tzu

导入语　Lead-in

孙子（约前545~约前470），字长卿，又称"孙武"或"孙武子"，春秋末期齐国乐安（今山东北部）人，中国著名军事家和政治家，被后世尊称为"兵家至圣"，也有"百世兵家之师"和"东方兵学鼻祖"之誉。他的传世之作《孙子兵法》始终为后世兵法家推崇，被誉为"兵学圣典"，已经成为最著名的兵学典范之书。孙子及其军事思想不但对后世兵家具有深远的影响，而且在世界军事史上也享有崇高的地位。孙子的思想早已超越军事领域，在政治、外交、经济、文化等方面都有广泛的影响。

 文化剪影 Cultural Outline

  Sun Tzu's Art of War, also known as *Sun Wu's Art of War* or *Sun Wu's Book of War*, consists of thirteen chapters. It is the earliest military works **extant**[①] in China and also the earliest book of war in the world, which is nearly two thousand three hundred and fifty years earlier than *The Theory on War* by Clausewitz. As the "Holy Classic of Military Science", it is not only an important part of China's fine traditional culture, but also a shining pearl in the world's military field.

  《孙子兵法》,又称《孙武兵法》或《孙武兵书》,有13篇。它是中国现存最早的军事著作,也是世界上最早的兵书,比克劳塞维茨的《战争论》早了将近2350年。作为"兵学圣典",它不仅是中国优秀传统文化的重要组成部分,也是世界军事领域的一颗璀璨明珠。

  Brimming with materialist thought, Sun Tzu not only believed in the objectivity of the existence of the world, but also took it for granted that everything in the world keeps moving and changing. Once published, *Sun Tzu's Art of War* shocked the world. His distinctive and profound ideas not only resonated with He Lv, King of Wu, but also were tested on the maids of honor, who were then transformed into **qualified**[②] soldiers. Later, leading thirty thousand soldiers to gallop for one thousand li, Sun Tzu conquered the capital of Chu in the west with a force inferior in number to win five victories on end, **overawed**[③] Qi and Chu in the north, and accomplished the great power of Wu.

孙子坚信唯物主义思想,他不仅相信世界是客观存在的,而且认为世界万物均在不断运动变化。《孙子兵法》一经问世便惊世骇俗,他独特深邃的见解不仅引发了吴王阖闾的共鸣,而且试于宫女,宫女成兵。后来,孙子用兵三万,千里奔驰,五战五捷,以少胜多,西破楚都,北威齐晋,成就了吴国霸业。

Sun Tzu's Art of War revealed some universal laws of military organization, established a complete system of military theory, and proposed that politics is the **principal**① factor to the outcome of war. In addition, the book embodied simple materialism, stressing that to conclude the tendency of war lies not in worshipping ghosts or gods but in measuring "moral justice, heavenly time, geographical location, general's orders and military discipline", and that the way to victory is not in static analysis but in **dynamic**② creation to take advantage of human subjective **initiative**③ and turn unfavorable into favorable.

《孙子兵法》揭示了一些排兵布阵的普遍规律,构建了一套完整的军事理论体系,书中还提出了政治是战争胜负的首要因素。此外,该书还体现了朴素的唯物主义思想,强调判断战争走向不在于拜鬼神,而在于权衡"道、天、地、将、法",制胜之道不在于静态分析,而在于动态创造,需要发挥人的主观能动性,化不利为有利。

 佳句点睛　Punchlines

1. Those skilled in war avoid the enemy when he is keen and attack him when he is **sluggish**① and his soldiers are homesick.

善用兵者，避其锐气，击其惰归。

2. Internationally renowned as "The First Ancient Book of War in the World", *Sun Tzu's Art of War* has now been translated into many languages.

《孙子兵法》在国际上被誉为"世界古代第一部兵书"，现在已被译成了多种语言。

3. Due to his rich and innovative philosophy in military science, Sun Tzu is listed as one of the "Three Shining Stars" in the late Spring and Autumn Period, along with Lao Tzu and Confucius.

由于军事科学方面丰富而创新的哲学思想，孙子被列为春秋末期的"三颗明星"之一，与老子和孔子并列。

 情景对话　Situational Dialogue

A: There're too many talented people. Which one should I write about?

B: Have you got an idea of Sun Tzu?

A: You mean Sun Tzu, in the late Spring and Autumn Period?

B: Yes. Sun Tzu is a great militarist and statesman.

A: A good idea. I've known quite a lot about him. He is often listed as one of the "Three Shining Stars" in philosophy before the Qin Dynasty.

B: Have you got an idea of Sun Tzu's contribution?

A: Of course. His greatest contribution is *Sun Tzu's Art of War*.

B: Could you introduce it for me?

A: OK. *Sun Tzu's Art of War* is honored as the "Holy Book of Military Science". It is, so to speak, full of sparkling ideas, penetrating and worthy of praise. For example, "A man who knows his enemy and himself will win a hundred battles" "It is the best of all to subdue the enemy with no war".

B: In this case, Sun Tzu was also a peace-loving militarist.

A: Well said. One of the reasons why great men are great is that they love peace.

A：才华出众的人太多了。我该写哪一位呢？

B：你知道孙子吗？

A：你是说春秋末期的孙子吗？

B：是的，他是一位伟大的军事家和政治家。

A：好主意。我对他了解挺多的，他常被列为秦朝前哲学界的"三颗明星"之一。

B：你知道孙子的贡献吗？

A: 当然知道,他最伟大的贡献就是《孙子兵法》。

B: 能给我介绍一下吗?

A: 好的,《孙子兵法》被誉为"兵学圣典",可以说这本书是字字珠玑、鞭辟入里、可圈可点,比如,"知彼知己,百战不殆""不战而屈人之兵,善之善者也"。

B: 这么说,孙子还是一位热爱和平的军事家喽。

A: 说得好!伟人之所以是伟人,其中一个原因就是他们热爱和平。

生词注解 Notes

① extant /ˈekstənt/ *adj.* 现存的;显著的

② qualified /ˈkwɒlɪfaɪd/ *adj.* 合格的;有资格的

③ overawe /ˌəʊvərˈɔː/ *vt.* 慑服;使……敬畏

④ principal /ˈprɪnsəpl/ *adj.* 主要的;最重要的

⑤ dynamic /daɪˈnæmɪk/ *adj.* 动态的;有活力的

⑥ initiative /ɪˈnɪʃətɪv/ *n.* 倡议;首创精神

⑦ sluggish /ˈslʌɡɪʃ/ *adj.* 迟钝的;懒惰的

第二部分 领袖人物

Part II Leading Figures

秦始皇

The First Emperor of Qin

导入语 Lead-in

秦始皇（前259～前210），姓嬴，名政，又称"祖龙"，出生于赵国都城邯郸。伟大的政治家、战略家、改革家，中华文明史上第一位皇帝。嬴政是秦庄襄王之子，十三岁登基，二十一岁亲政，除奸权，重贤能，并吞六国，统一中国，建立秦朝，称"始皇帝"；其后大胆改革，锐意进取，废分封制，行郡县制，建官僚制，统一度量衡，北修长城，南征百越，修筑灵渠，沟通水系，一生五次巡游治国理政，殚精竭虑，最后一次巡游时驾崩于沙丘宫。他奠定了中国两千多年政治制度的基本格局，开创了一个中央集权封建专制的新时代。

文化剪影 Cultural Outline

The First Emperor of Qin was the first to claim himself Emperor, established the first **centralized**①, unified, multi-ethnic feudal state in the history of world civilization, laid the foundation of the basic political system of China for more than two thousand years and was praised as "The First Emperor throughout the Ages". He unified China, conquered all the southern ethnic groups, and attacked the northern **nomadic**② tribes; and he migrated people to **consolidate**③ the northern border regions, connected the southwestern areas, expanded the territory and promoted the ethnic integration.

秦始皇首称皇帝,建立了世界文明史上第一个中央集权的、统一的、多民族的封建制国家,奠定了中国两千余年基本政治制度的基础,被誉为"千古一帝"。他一统天下,南征百越,北击匈奴,迁徙人口,巩固北疆,连通西南,开疆拓土,促进民族融合。

The First Emperor of Qin's greatness lies not just in political and military aspects, but more in economy. He **launched**④ a series of reforms and in measuring, monetary and traffic systems. The integration and unification of the three systems made there be national standards for the first time in the whole China, which not only sped up the economic development, but also strengthened the centralized **regime**⑤.

秦始皇的丰功伟绩不仅体现在政治和军事方面,更多地体现在经济方面。他在度量衡、货币和交通体系三个方面发起了一系列改革。三种体制的整合统一让整个华夏第一次出现了国家标准,这不仅加速了经济发展,而且强化了中央政权。

The First Emperor of Qin was the **initiator**① of the Chinese feudal society over two thousand years. Besides his great military, political and economic feats during his reign, he made some other national standards in culture and society. His word to unify and simplify Chinese characters was not only beneficial to teach and **cultivate**② the people, but also a good reform of writing system, laying a sound foundation for the later formation and development of the regular script.

秦始皇是中国两千多年封建社会的创立者。主政期间,除了文治武功和经济上的丰功伟绩,他还在文化和社会方面制定了国家标准。他下令统一并简化汉字,不仅有利于教化国人,而且也是对书写体系的改良,为后来楷书的形成和发展奠定了坚实的基础。

佳句点睛　Punchlines

1. I am the first emperor, from which later generations can count the second, the third, and the ten thousandth, handing it down to eternity.
朕为始皇帝。后世以计数,二世三世至于万世,传之无穷。

2. The story that began with the sword must end with the sword.
这个由剑开始的故事必将用剑来终结。

3. When I'm alive, I shall defend the lands, pioneer the frontiers, pacify the barbarians, and lay the foundation for Qin of ten thousand generations. When I die, I shall turn my body into the dragon soul to bless my Huaxia forever.

朕在，当守土开疆，扫平四夷，定我大秦万世之基！朕亡，亦将身化龙魂，佑我华夏永世不衰！

情景对话 Situational Dialogue

A: Do you think it necessary to learn about history?

B: Of course. The ancients said that a copper mirror rights your clothes, a historical mirror shows you rise and fall, and a human mirror tells you gains and losses.

A: Do you know how long the Chinese feudal society lasted?

B: Dating from the Qin Dynasty founded in 221 BC, it had lasted for over 2,100 years.

A: Can you tell me who it was that founded the feudal dynasty, then?

B: The First Emperor of Qin.

A: What do you think about him?

B: I think he was one of the great monarchs in the world because his centralized monarchy was the first in the human history of civilization.

A: I agree with you. Anyone who can make it first is worthy of respect and admiration. But I admire him for something else.

B: What do you mean?

A: His greatness was that he made many national standards and left behind a kind of "standard **consciousness**®".

B: What do you mean by "national standards"?

A: The **standardized**® roads, vehicles, characters, and weights and measures.

B: I see. Behind the standards are countless scientific inventions. No wonder the Qin Dynasty was great.

A: 你认为有必要了解历史吗?

B: 当然有必要。古人云:铜镜正衣冠,史镜明兴衰,人镜知得失。

A: 你知道中国的封建社会持续了多长时间吗?

B: 从前221年秦朝建国算起,持续了2100多年。

A: 你能告诉我当时是谁建立了这个封建王朝吗?

B: 是秦始皇。

A: 你对他有什么看法?

B: 我认为,嬴政是世界上伟大的君主之一,因为他的中央集权政体是人类文明史上的第一个君主政体。

A: 我同意。任何首创之人都值得尊敬和钦佩。但是,我钦佩他却另有其因。

B: 此话怎讲?

A: 他的伟大之处在于他制定了很多国家标准,并留下了一种

"标准意识"。

B: 你说的"国家标准"是什么意思？

A: 就是标准的道路、车辆、文字和度量衡。

B: 我明白了。这些标准引出了数不清的科学发明。难怪秦朝是一个伟大的王朝。

生词注解 Notes

① centralized /ˈsentrəlaɪzd/ *adj.* 中央集权的

② nomadic /nəʊˈmædɪk/ *adj.* 游牧的；游动的

③ consolidate /kənˈsɒlɪdeɪt/ *vt.* 巩固；使……固定

④ launch /lɔːntʃ/ *vt.* 发起；发动

⑤ regime /reɪˈʒiːm/ *n.* 政体；社会制度

⑥ initiator /ɪˈnɪʃɪeɪtə(r)/ *n.* 创始者；发起人

⑦ cultivate /ˈkʌltɪveɪt/ *vt.* 培养；陶冶

⑧ consciousness /ˈkɒnʃəsnəs/ *n.* 意识；觉悟

⑨ standardized /ˈstændədaɪzd/ *adj.* 标准的；标准化的

汉武帝

Emperor Wu of Han

 导入语 Lead-in

汉武帝（前156～前87），本名刘彻，幼名刘彘，陕西长安（今西安）人，汉朝第七位皇帝，伟大的政治家、战略家、改革家和文学家。生于长安未央宫，为汉景帝之子。汉武帝大胆改革，设察举制选贤任能，中央设内外朝制，地方设刺史制、行推恩令，削王权增帝权，强化中央集权，对内实施经济文化垄断，对外征伐四方、开辟丝绸之路。他的雄才大略和文治武功，使汉朝成为当时世界上最强大的国家。汉武帝创立了年号，是中国第一位使用年号的皇帝。他开创了西汉王朝最繁荣的鼎盛时期，也是中国封建王朝的第一个发展高峰。

文化剪影 Cultural Outline

Emperor Wu of Han was a man of great talents and strategies throughout his life, and deserved the title of a great emperor. Politically, based on the traditional "three dukes and nine ministers" system, he designed the central court system made up of the emperor's cronies, which reinforced the emperor's authority; initiated cishi to supervise local **despots**① and government officials; issued a Grace-pushing Act to weaken the power of local **vassal**②; and adopted the recommendatory system to select and appoint virtuous talents, which expanded the base of governance. He adhered to the policy of external expansion, defeated Xiongnu, **subdued**③ the Western Regions, **annexed**④ Korea, exploited Nanyue and established the Han territory, so there emerged a powerful feudal cmpire with an unprecedented territory.

汉武帝一生雄才大略，堪称一代大帝。政治上，他四管齐下，在传统的"三公九卿"制的基础上设立中朝制，由皇帝亲信组成，加强了皇权；首创刺史，监督地方豪强官吏；颁布推恩令，削弱地方诸侯王权；建立察举制，唯才是举，选贤任能，扩大了统治基础。他坚持对外扩张政策，击溃匈奴，降服西域，吞并朝鲜，开拓南越，奠定了汉朝版图，缔造出一个疆域空前的强大封建帝国。

On the basis of the "Rule of Wen and Jing", Emperor Wu of Han carried out daring reforms and expanded the territory of the Han Dynasty.

During his reign, the dynasty is the most powerful and prosperous and forms the first peak development in the Chinese feudal history. Going with a series of westward **expeditions**⑤ and successive victories, Emperor Wu of Han sent Zhang Qian on diplomatic missions twice to the Western Regions, which opened up the Silk Road, made China put its vision turn to the world for the first time, pioneered the world journey of the Chinese civilization and promoted the **convergence**⑥ and prosperity of world civilizations.

汉武帝继承"文景之治",大胆改革,开疆拓土。他在位期间是汉朝最强盛的时期,也成为中国封建社会第一个发展高峰。伴随着一系列西征探险和不断胜利,汉武帝两次派张骞出使西域,开辟了丝绸之路,第一次将中国的目光投向世界,开辟了中华文明的世界征程,促进了世界文明的交汇和繁荣发展。

Emperor Wu of Han paid special attention to cultural construction and left many initiative measures in the history of Chinese culture: He set up the grand-scale national library, issued Taichu Calendar (first national calendar), initiated Taixue (imperial college) and established the Music Bureau, forming the situation of cultural governance of respecting Confucianism and obeying laws and laying a solid foundation of talents for the great political and military achievements but also for the brilliant diplomatic contributions.

汉武帝特别重视文化建设,在中国文化史上留下了诸多首创举措:设立规模宏大的国家图书馆、颁布太初历、创立太学、建乐府,形

成了尊儒守法的文治局面,为丰功伟绩和辉煌外交奠定了坚实的人才基础。

佳句点睛 Punchlines

1. Liu Che was not only a great statesman with outstanding abilities, but also a poet who loved literature and advocated cifu.

刘彻不仅是一位雄才大略的政治家,也是一位爱好文学、提倡辞赋的诗人。

2. Emperor Wu of Han **initiated**① the imperial college and the rural schools and established the system of selecting virtuous officials, which formed the unique civil service system in China.

汉武帝创建太学、乡学,设立举贤制度,形成了中国独特的文官制度。

3. The loss of son in later years and defeat in the military affairs seriously dampened Emperar Wu of Han's spirit.

晚年丧子和军事上的失利,严重打击了汉武帝的精神。

情景对话 Situational Dialogue

A: What do you think of Emperor Wu of Han, Jon?

B: He was one of the outstanding monarchs.

A: How outstanding on earth?

B: He started the most powerful and prosperous period of the Han Dynasty and made the first peak development of the feudal society of China. According to *The Records of the Historian*, he won countless victories against foreign invaders, carried out a series of successful reforms and **blazed**⑧ a new era.

A: His military victories allowed him to build an **unprecedented**⑨ empire and opened up the "Silk Road", which spread the story of China among the Asian, European and African continents for the first time. But, what do you mean by a new era?

B: Emperor Wu of Han said that "an unusual work must be waiting for unusual people." And only in a new era can there be unusual talented people who would like to devote themselves to the country and achieve the "unusual work".

A: Oh, I see. His interior reforms should be closely related to the "new era".

B: Emperor Wu of Han made so many innovative measures in order to make his times full of visions and vitality, and he made it.

A: 乔恩，你对汉武帝有什么看法？

B: 他是杰出的统治者之一。

A: 究竟有多杰出？

B: 他开启了汉朝最繁荣强盛的时期，创造了中国封建社会的第一个发展巅峰。据《史记》记载，他打败了不计其数的外来侵略者，实行了一系列成功的改革,创造了新纪元。

A: 军事胜利让他建立了史无前例的大帝国,开辟了"丝绸之路",让中国故事第一次在亚、欧、非三大洲之间得到传播。可是,你说的"新纪元"作何解释呢?

B: 汉武帝说过:"非常之功,必待非常之人。"只有身处新纪元,才会有非凡的人才愿意报效国家,取得"非常之功"。

A: 噢,我明白了。他的内部改革应该与"新纪元"密切相关。

B: 为了让当时的社会充满生机活力,汉武帝大胆改革创新。而且,他做到了。

生词注解 Notes

① despot /ˈdespɒt/ n. 豪强;暴君

② vassal /ˈvæsl/ n. 诸侯;封臣

③ subdue /səbˈdjuː/ vt. 制服;征服

④ annex /ˈæneks/ vt. 并吞;占为己有

⑤ expedition /ˌekspəˈdɪʃn/ n. 远征;探险

⑥ convergence /kənˈvɜːdʒəns/ n. 交汇;汇聚

⑦ initiate /ɪˈnɪʃieɪt/ vt. 创始;发起

⑧ blaze /bleɪz/ vt. 开辟

⑨ unprecedented /ʌnˈpresɪdentɪd/ adj. 空前的;史无前例的

隋文帝

Emperor Wen of Sui

导入语 Lead-in

隋文帝(541~604),本名杨坚,弘农郡华阴(今陕西华阴)人,隋朝开国皇帝,著名政治家、改革家、军事家。生于豪门世族,言寡、心孝、性严,入太学,十五岁封大将军,军事卓异,随周武帝平齐,政治出众,辅政北周,四十岁夺权建隋。称帝后,并西梁、灭南陈、平江南、破突厥,一统天下,励精图治,领均田令,设置粮仓,改革货币,选贤任能,巩固集权,强国富民,厉行节俭,结束了西晋以来将近三百年的社会动荡,在力求巩固国家统一的大政方针下,各方面都成就非凡,开创了光华璀璨的开皇盛世。

文化剪影　Cultural Outline

Emperor Wen of Sui ended nearly three hundred years of wars and disputes in the Western Jin Dynasty, restored the tradition of "Great Unity" among the Chinese people, opened up the glorious "Rule of Emperor Kai", giving people a **respite**① to live and work in peace and **contentment**②. He started lots of political measures, followed by later dynasties such as Tang and Song. He further consolidated the unification of the north and the south, defeated the arrogance of the nomadic people, maintained peace on the border and stabilized the situation of East Asia.

隋文帝结束了西晋以来近三百年的战乱纷争,恢复了中华民族"大一统"的传统,开创了辉煌的"开皇之治",人民得以休养生息,安居乐业。他创立了许多政治措施,为唐、宋等后朝仿效。他进一步巩固了南北统一局面,打击了游牧民族的嚣张气焰,维护了边境和平,稳定了东亚局势。

Emperor Wen of Sui restored the "Great Unity", so there emerged the Sui System that the system of "Three Councils and Six Ministries" were **implemented**③ in the Central Government and the "Province-County" two-level administration changed from the "Province-Prefecture-County" three-level administration in local affairs, which simplified institutions and improved **efficiency**④, and meanwhile saved governmental expenditures, relieved people's burdens, strengthened feudal centralization and promoted social stability.

隋文帝恢复"大一统",故有"隋制",中央实行"三省六部"制度,地方改"州郡县"三级管理为"州县"两级管理,精简了机构,提高了效率,同时节省了政府开支,减轻了人民负担,加强了封建中央集权,促进了社会稳定。

Emperor Wen of Sui built the commercial **metropolis**⑤ of Daxing (Xi'an now), where the royal palace, the royal town and the dwelling houses were clearly defined and the streets and lanes were designed in order, which changed the disorderly and **unsymmetrical**⑥ capital layout in the past and formed a balanced and symmetrical urban construction style, starting its course to be one of the "World's Four Great Ancient Capitals of Civilization". In ethnical relations, the eastern Turkic were sincerely convinced to get annexed into the Sui Dynasty, honoring him as "Saint Khan". The most distinctive is perhaps his act of abolishing the "Nine-Grade Ranking System" and adopting the "Imperial Examinations" to select officials, which made everyone able to serve the country by passing the tests and expanded the ruling foundation.

隋文帝建设商都大兴城(今西安),皇宫、皇城和民居界限分明,大街小巷整齐划一,一改过去杂乱无章的都城布局,形成了平衡对称的城市建设风格,开始了"世界四大文明古都"的发展历程。在民族关系上,东突厥心悦诚服并入隋朝,把隋文帝誉为"圣人可汗"。隋文帝最具特色的改革或许是废"九品中正"、兴"科举",人人都可通过考

试报效国家,扩大了统治基础。

佳句点睛 Punchlines

1. I heard that the law of heaven is impartial but gives priority to virtues, and looking through the emperors and kings of the previous generations, no one can rule long for luxury.

我闻天道无亲,唯德是与,历观前代帝王,未有奢华而能长久者。

2. People have got descendants, who can have no affection for them? For the lands under heaven, affection should be cut away.

人生子孙,谁不爱念,既为天下,事须割情。

3. To earn fame, it is enough to get one historical book, why erect a monument? If the **descendants**① cannot protect the families, it can be just used as others' chart weights.

欲求名,一卷史书足矣,何用碑为? 若子孙不能保家,徒与人作镇石耳。

情景对话 Situational Dialogue

A: Do you know Wen Tianxiang?

B: Wen Tianxiang is a national hero.

A: He was the first in the imperial civil examination. Do you know which dynasty the system of imperial examinations come from?

B: I do know nothing about it. I just know it was a major means to select officials in ancient times.

A: It originates from the Sui Dynasty. Emperor Wen of Sui abolished the "Nine-Grade Ranking" System since the Wei Dynasty and initiated the "Imperial Examination" System.

B: I know this emperor, who got a historic feat — the "Rule of Emperor Kai". Right?

A: Yes. He really initiated many institutions. Many great achievements in the prosperous Tang were inseparable from learning the Sui system.

B: In this case, Emperor Wen of Sui was really an influential historical figure.

A: The imperial civil examination system, for example, was **abolished**⑧ only in 1905 and lasted through all **subsequent**⑨ feudal dynasties.

B: You really know everything.

A: 你知道文天祥吗?

B: 文天祥是位民族英雄。

A: 他还是科举考试第一名呢。你知道科举考试源于哪个朝代吗?

B: 这我还真不知道,只知道这是古代选拔官员的主要手段。

A: 它源于隋朝。隋文帝废除了曹魏以来的"九品中正"制,首创了"科举"制。

B: 我知道这位皇帝,他的历史功绩叫"开皇之治",对吧?

A: 是的。他的确有许多制度创举。盛唐有很多了不起的成就都离不开学习隋制。

B: 这么说,隋文帝还真是一位有影响的历史人物。

A: 以科举制为例,这项制度贯穿了其后的所有封建王朝,直到1905年才被废除。

B: 你真是无所不通啊。

生词注解 Notes

① respite /ˈrespaɪt/　*n.* 短暂的休息;缓解

② contentment /kənˈtentmənt/　*n.* 幸福感;满意

③ implement /ˈɪmplɪment/　*vt.* 实施;执行

④ efficiency /ɪˈfɪʃnsɪ/　*n.* 效率;效能

⑤ metropolis /məˈtrɒpəlɪs/　*n.* 大都市;首府

⑥ unsymmetrical /ˌʌnsɪˈmetrɪkl/　*adj.* 非对称的;不匀称的

⑦ descendant /dɪˈsendənt/　*n.* 后代

⑧ abolish /əˈbɒlɪʃ/　*vt.* 废除;废止

⑨ subsequent /ˈsʌbsɪkwənt/　*adj.* 随后的;后续的

唐太宗

Emperor Taizong of Tang

导入语 Lead-in

唐太宗(598~649),本名李世民,陇西成纪(今甘肃秦安)人。他是唐朝第二位皇帝,杰出的政治家、战略家、军事家、诗人。唐太宗生于陕西武功,唐高祖次子,少从军,擅长骑,有救驾之功,倡晋阳起兵,率军灭隋,后四方征战封秦王。经玄武门之变,成为太子,禅登宝座,既往不咎,知人善任,从谏如流,完善制度,以隋为鉴,励精图治,河清海晏,轻徭役,尚节俭,对外用兵,威名远播,创"贞观之治",夜不闭户,道不拾遗。唐太宗采取怀柔的政治手段有效解决了民族问题,促进了民族团结和国家统一。

文化剪影　Cultural Outline

During the reign of Emperor Taizong of Tang, it was known as the "Rule of Zhengguan" in history for its social **stability**①, economic prosperity, prominent military achievements, ethnic integration and harmonious relationships from all directions. Politically, "basing the Tang System on the Sui System", he bettered the system of three provinces and six ministries, going on to strengthen feudal centralization. In governance, he selected and appointed the virtuous and talented, accepted wise advice and let everybody fully display his talents. Economically, he lessened **corvee**②, cut taxes and punished **prudently**③, so the people enjoyed a stable life; he valued commerce and made the "Silk Road" opened up by the Han Dynasty an golden corridor in the world. In military aspects, he unified the whole country and established a feudal empire with an unprecedented territory.

唐太宗在位期间,社会稳定,经济繁荣,军力强盛,民族融合,八方咸服,史称"贞观之治"。他在政治上实行"隋规唐随",完善三省六部制,继续加强中央集权;在管理上选贤任能,从谏如流,使得人尽其才;在经济上轻徭役、薄赋税、慎刑罚,人民生活安定,商业发展,使汉朝开辟的"丝绸之路"发展成为一条世界性的黄金走廊;在军事上统一全国,建立了疆域空前的封建帝国。

Emperor Taizong of Tang got his own ways to **recruit**④ virtuous people and he was expert in discovering talents and putting them on suitable positions. Before coming into power, he established a Literature Institute in his King Qin's Mansion to collect talents for reference anytime. After taking the throne, he first set up a Hongwen Institute to reserve talents for the country. He then learned from the Sui system and stuck to the Imperial Civic Examination system to select **competent**[5] people with no regards to their family status, which greatly added the chance to earn fame to poor people. In addition, Emperor Taizong of Tang was broad-minded and took into no consideration the past **grievance**[6]; he made bold use of former political opponents and surrendering personage. During the reign of Emperor Taizong, there was a wealth of talents and political harmony.

唐太宗募贤有道,知人善任。即位前,在秦王府设文学馆,收揽人才,以备随时咨询,即位后,一设弘文馆,为天下储备英才。二学习隋制,坚持科举制,不问门第选拔人才,大大增加寒门子弟谋取功名的机会。此外,唐太宗胸襟开阔,不计前嫌,大胆启用政敌旧部和投诚人士。唐太宗在位期间,人才济济,政通人和。

Emperor Taizong of Tang had been world-famous for his civil governance and military feats for ages. During his twenty three years of sincere and **industrious**[7] efforts, he established a great empire with an unprecedented territory, where there was not only harmonious coexistence of various ethnic groups but also fruitful cultural exchanges between the east and the west. In terms of ethnic relations, he adhered to the idea to take the world as a family, spreading power and virtue far-away, inviting people with kindness and honesty, and treating ethnic groups with affection and respect, so he was respected as "Heavenly Khan" by the states in the West Regions. He pursued the **placatory**® and opening policy and actively developed trade and commerce, making the "Silk Road" a road of cultural exchanges between the east and the west while the Tang people have taken root in the countries along the roads and have been the representative name of the Chinese nation.

多年来,唐太宗一直因其文治武功而闻名于世。二十三年励精图治,他建立了一个疆域空前的大帝国,不仅使不同民族和谐共存,而且东西方文化交流硕果累累。在民族关系上,他坚持天下为家的理念,威德致远,慈厚怀人,亲尊待夷,被西域诸国尊为"天可汗"。他推行怀柔开放的政策,积极发展商贸,将"丝绸之路"变成一条东西方文化交流之路,唐人在沿路国家扎根下来,成为中华民族的代名词。

佳句点睛　Punchlines

1. Nothing goes far but majesty and virtue and nothing invites people but kindness and honesty.

非威德无以致远,非慈厚无以怀人。

2. Do not use a man not for his humility; do not respect a man not for his insult.

不以卑而不用,不以辱而不尊。

3. The idea worth viewing, do not criticize its arguing; the theory worth adopting, do not blame its writing.

其义可观,不责其辩;其理可用,不责其文。

 情景对话 Situational Dialogue

A: There're three mirrors in life. Do you know what they are?

B: I remember Emperor Taizong of Tang said, "A copper mirror rights your clothes, a historical mirror shows you rise and fall, and a human mirror tells you gains and losses."

A: Good memory.

B: What do you think of the emperor?

A: I think he was first of all a great statesman because he established an empire larger than any other former dynasties and turned the "Silk Road" from trade and commerce to cultural exchange and coexistence. Secondly, I think he was an outstanding military strategist because without **transcendental**① military gifts he couldn't spread his majesty and virtues far away.

B: I agree with you. Genghis Khan said, "He who wants to bring peace and stability to the kingdom must be familiar with Emperor Taizong of Tang's Art of War." Mao Zedong praised, "Since ancient times, there has never been a better man than Li Shimin in military affairs."

A: It stands to reason.

A: 人生有三面镜子,你知道这三面镜子是什么吗?

B: 我记得唐太宗说过:"夫以铜为镜,可以正衣冠;以古为镜,可以知兴替;以人为镜,可以明得失。"

A: 好记性。

B: 你对这位皇帝有何看法?

A: 我认为他首先是一位伟大的政治家,因为他建立了一个疆域空前辽阔的帝国,并把"丝绸之路"从商贸之路发展为文化交流与共存之路。其次,我认为他是一位杰出的军事战略家,如果没有卓越的军事天赋,他很难威德致远。

B: 我同意你的看法。成吉思汗说过:"欲安邦定国者,必悉唐宗兵法。"毛泽东称赞说:"自古能军无出李世民之右者。"

A: 言之有理。

生词注解 Notes

① stability /stəˈbɪlətɪ/ n. 稳定;稳定性

② corvee /kɔrˈve/ n. 徭役

③ prudently /ˈpruːdntlɪ/ adv. 谨慎地;慎重地

④ recruit /rɪˈkruːt/ vt. 征募;聘用

⑤ competent /ˈkɒmpɪtənt/ adj. 有能力的;能干的

⑥ grievance /ˈɡriːvəns/ n. 不平;冤情

⑦ industrious /ɪnˈdʌstrɪəs/ adj. 勤勉的;繁忙的

⑧ placatory /pləˈkeɪtərɪ/ adj. 怀柔的;抚慰的

⑨ transcendental /ˌtrænsenˈdentl/ adj. 超越的;超自然的

成吉思汗

Genghis Khan

导入语 Lead-in

成吉思汗(1162～1227),元太祖,姓孛儿只斤,名铁木真,蒙古族乞颜部人。杰出的军事家、政治家。生于漠北斡难河(今蒙古国肯特省),九岁父汗遇害,颠沛流离,十八岁败蔑儿乞人当上乞颜部可汗,后联合王汗打败扎木和蒙古贵族联军,灭王汗、蛮部太阳汗,会盟于斡南河(今鄂嫩河),被蒙古诸王和群臣尊为"成吉思汗",成立大蒙古国。在位二十二年期间,先后征伐西夏、西辽、金国和花剌子模,统一部落。成吉思汗一生共经历六十多次战争,除了十三翼之战因实力悬殊而主动撤退之外,都大获全胜。他倡导领户分封,创建蒙古文字。马克思评价说:"成吉思汗戎马倥偬,征战终生,统一了蒙古,为中国统一而战。"

文化剪影　Cultural Outline

Genghis Khan was a world-famous militarist. He had a carefree childhood but a hard boyhood because his father was murdered, bullied by other tribes to the fullest extent; however, with his unyielding character, firm **perseverance**[①] and outstanding military talents, he recaptured the Khan of the Kyan tribe at his twenty-two years. Thereafter, he waged wars in the prairie desert and unified all of the Mongolian tribes within twenty years. And at the age of forty-four, he called upon all the tribe chieftains for a political conference at the Onon River source, where he was respected as Genghis Khan. During his reign, he waged wars around each year and even carried out several wars at the same time, but he direct military operations with miraculous skills; he utterly defeated Jin and wiped out Khwarezm, Xiliao and Xixia successively. At the time of his death in 1227, there were still three wills left behind, by which Jin was **eliminated**[②].

成吉思汗是世界著名的军事家。童年无忧无虑,少时因为父亲被害而生活艰难,饱受其他部落欺凌,然而他不屈不挠,坚韧不拔,军事才华出众,二十二岁时夺回乞颜部可汗之位。其后,他征战草原大漠,历经二十年统一了蒙古,四十四岁时,会盟蒙古各部落首领于斡难河河源,被尊为成吉思汗。在位期间,他四处用兵,连年征伐,甚至同时向多方开战,但他用兵如神,先后击溃金国,灭掉花剌子模、西辽和西夏。1227年去世时,仍有三条遗嘱留世,借此灭了金国。

Throughout his life, Genghis Khan lived through over sixty battles and destroyed forty countries and in the end unified the whole Mongolia, which avoided the situation that the weak are the prey of the strong among the tribes who no longer killed one another for ranches, livestock and slaves, laid a solid foundation for his descendants who established an empire crossing Europe and Asia; the empire almost joined up the whole Asia and opened up a continental channel from the Pacific Ocean to the Baltic Sea and from the Persian Gulf to Siberia, where people could move at will.

　　成吉思汗一生历经了六十多场战役，灭四十国，最终统一了蒙古，避免了各个部落之间的弱肉强食，国家间不再因为争夺牧场、牲畜和奴隶而相互杀戮，为后代建立横跨亚欧大陆的帝国奠定了基础，帝国从太平洋到波罗的海，从波斯湾到西伯利亚，几乎联合了整个亚洲，开辟了洲际通道，人民可以自由往来。

　　The Mongolian **aristocrats**③ led by Genghis Khan conquering the world, they adopted a comparatively **liberal**④ religious policy; they did not force the subdued to convert to their own Shamanism but advocated religious freedom and **inclusiveness**⑤ and allowed Mongolian people to join various religious sects. All kinds of religions developed respectively, all the ethnic minorities integrated gradually and stabilized the political rule. After Kublai Khan, grandson of Genghis Khan, unified the whole China, Genghis Khan was respected as "Emperor Taizu of Yuan".

成吉思汗领导的蒙古贵族征服天下的同时,采用了比较开明的宗教政策,不是迫使被征服者改信蒙古人的萨满教,而是倡导宗教自由和兼容并蓄,而且允许蒙古人参加各种教派。各种宗教得以各自发展,各民族得以渐渐融合,稳定了政治统治。成吉思汗的孙子忽必烈可汗统一全中国后,将成吉思汗尊为"元太祖"。

佳句点睛 Punchlines

1. Don't care how far you can go; just go ahead and the goal will be surely reached. Don't be afraid of danger or difficulty; try and you will succeed.

不要理会能走多远,只管前进,目标必会到达;不要害怕险阻,尝试便会成功。

2. Once I get the wise and the able, I'll let them follow me and not go far.

一旦我得到贤士和能人,就让他们紧随我,不让远去。

3. Neither expect to be protected nor beg for justice. Only by learning to survive with your own strength can you be a true Mongol anyone cannot beat off the horse.

不要寄希望于有人保护你,不要乞求有人替你主持公道。只有学会靠自己的力量活下来,你才算是真正的蒙古人,任何人都打不落马的蒙古人。

情景对话 Situational Dialogue

A: Could you tell me what the secret of Genghis Khan's victory was?

B: Discipline and **ambition**⑥, because he said, "Without iron discipline, the **chariot**⑦ cannot go far. Your horse can gallop as far as your heart is wide."

A: Genghis Khan is said to have lived through over sixty battles with only one lost. His military victories resulted in the founding of the Great Mongolia.

B: Where there is a will, there is a way.

A: He also said, "Once I get the wise and the able, I'll let them follow me and not go far."

B: If you are thirsty for talents, you will get plenty of help. It is natural and smooth for Genghis Khan to unify the Mongolian tribes.

A: Certainly.

A: 你能告诉我成吉思汗取胜的秘诀是什么吗？

B: 纪律和雄心，他说过："没有铁的纪律，战车就开不远。你的心胸有多宽广，你的战马就能驰骋多远。"

A: 据说成吉思汗身经六十余战，只有一次失利。他凭借骁勇善战建立了大蒙古国。

B: 有志者，事竟成嘛。

A: 他还说过:"一旦我得到贤士和能人,就让他们紧随我,不让远去。"

B: 求贤若渴,得道多助。成吉思汗统一蒙古,自然是水到渠成、顺理成章了。

A: 这话没错。

生词注解　Notes

① perseverance /ˌpɜːsɪˈvɪərəns/　*adj.* 毅力;韧性

② eliminate /ɪˈlɪmɪneɪt/　*vt.* 消除;排除

③ aristocrat /ˈærɪstəkræt/　*n.* 贵族

④ liberal /ˈlɪbərəl/　*adj.* 开明的;不拘泥的

⑤ inclusiveness /ɪnˈkluːsɪvnəs/　*n.* 包容;包容性

⑥ ambition /æmˈbɪʃn/　*n.* 雄心;野心

⑦ chariot /ˈtʃærɪət/　*n.*(古代用于战斗或比赛的)双轮敞篷马车

康熙皇帝

Emperor Kangxi

导入语　Lead-in

康熙（1654～1722），本名爱新觉罗·玄烨，清朝第四位皇帝。杰出的政治家、战略家、军事家,中国历史上在位时间最长的君王。康熙是顺治帝第三子,少年勤学不倦,八岁成少年天子,十四岁亲政,十六岁除权臣鳌拜,掌管朝廷,多次巡查全国,整吏治,亲百姓,先后平三藩,收台湾,战雅克萨驱逐沙俄,西征漠北、多伦会盟、怀柔蒙古各部,积极开展对外关系,加强中央集权,注意休养生息,发展经济,治吏亲民,坚定捍卫统一的多民族国家,奠定了清朝兴盛的根基,开创了康乾盛世的大好局面。

文化剪影　Cultural Outline

Emperor Kangxi, diligent in political governance, made extraordinary achievements; he was the founder of the "Kang-Qian Flourishing Ages" and a powerful guardian of the feudal monarchy. He not only **consolidated**① his imperial power by weakening the authority of the outer court and the Manchu Nobility Assembly, but also **alleviated**② the serious contradiction between Man and Han. He insisted on learning the Han culture and giving priority to **indoctrination**③ rather than decrees. In addition, Kangxi valued inspection across the land. He toured the south six times, the east three times and the west once, and inspected hundreds of times around the **environs**④ of Beijing and the Mongolian area.

康熙皇帝勤政，成就非凡，是"康乾盛世"的奠基人和封建帝制的有力捍卫者，不仅通过削弱外廷和满族贵族大会的权威巩固了帝权，而且缓和了严重的满汉矛盾。他坚持学习汉文化，优先考虑教化而非法令。此外，康熙还重视巡察全国，曾南巡六次、东巡三次、西巡一次，巡视京畿和蒙古达数百次。

Faced with the Rebellions of the Three **Seigniors**⑤, Kangxi attacked resolutely; he recovered the lost territory of six provinces and wiped out the separatist forces within five years. In the face the **secession**⑥ of Taiwan, he recovered it decisively; within one year, Taiwan was returned to the administration of Fujian Province. Confronted with Russia's endless invasions of the Heilongjiang River reaches, Kangxi staunchly counterattacked and **annihilated**⑦ nearly all of the Russian soldiers in the second Battle of Jaxa, forcing Russia to sign *The Treaty of Nerchinsk*, which **stipulated**⑧ that the south of the Outer Hinggan Mountains and the north of the Heilongjiang River as well as the east of the Ussuri River all belonged to China and brought about the close-to-170-year peace in the area. Seeing the Junggar chaos in Mongolia, Kangxi eradicated its leader Galdon mercilessly and brought Mobei Mongolia into the domain of China.

面对三藩之乱，康熙坚决打击，先后收复六省失地，五年内消灭了分裂势力。面对台湾割据，康熙坚决收复，历时一年，将台湾归治于福建。面对沙俄无休止的入侵黑龙江流域，康熙坚决回击，第二次雅克萨之战几乎全歼俄军，迫其缔结《尼布楚条约》，规定外兴安岭以南、黑龙江以北，乌苏里江以东均为中国领土，为该地区带来了近一百七十年的和平安定。面对准噶尔祸乱蒙古，康熙坚决铲除其首领噶尔丹，将漠北蒙古纳入了中国版图。

Emperor Kangxi not only excelled in diligence, but also learned to perfect himself. He could inspire all efforts to keep the country prosperous and stable, gaining respect and support of the masses deeply. Kangxi was never bored with learning and was open-minded. This tolerance and kindness led him to adopt an enlightened ethnic policy and value the Han literati. He paid homage to Xiaoling Mausoleum of Ming in

Nanjing and Confucius's Temple in Qufu, Shangdong, which was not only **conducive**① to easing ethnic hatred, but also to promoting cultural construction and academic development.

　　康熙皇帝不仅勤政,而且力求自我完善。他竭尽所能维护国家繁荣稳定,深受百姓的尊敬和爱戴。康熙学而不厌、思想开明,这种包容和仁慈让他采取开明的民族政策,重用汉族文人。他拜谒南京的明孝陵和山东曲阜的孔庙,这不仅有利于缓和民族仇恨,而且有利于促进文化建设和学术发展。

佳句点睛　Punchlines

1. In the supreme reign, we should not focus on laws and regulations, but on education.

　　至治之世,不以法令为亟,而以教化为先。

2. The principle of learning should be with no interruption. Never stop halfway.

　　学问之道,宜无间断。其勿辍。

3. I have started to study since five years old. Reading aloud very often till midnight, I am delighted and never tired.

　　朕自五龄受书。诵读恒至夜分,乐此不为疲也。

情景对话 Situational Dialogue

A: What shall we talk about today?

B: Can you tell me which emperor ruled the longest in Chinese history?

A: It's Emperor Kangxi, Aisingioro Xuanye, the fourth emperor of Qing. Who had taken the throne for sixty-one years.

B: What is the most impressive thing about him?

A: His greatness should be nothing but his glorious political and military achievements. You know he was not only a pioneer of the "Kang-Qian Flourishing Ages" but also an outstanding representative of firmly safeguarding the system of unified multi-ethnic country.

B: What's the reason for that?

A: There are two reasons I think very important. One is his responsibility of state and history. He said, "If we do not take care of a matter, we'll plague the whole country; if we do not understand a matter, we'll bring calamity for a hundred years."

B: The emperor was noted for his diligent governance. And what is the other?

A: The other is his **approach**① to employ talented people. He said, "National employment should be based on virtues and then on talents."

B: I agree with you. But what I'm most impressed is his way of reading.

A: It seems that reading and governing cannot be separated.

A: 今天我们讨论什么呢？

B: 你能告诉我中国历史上哪位皇帝的统治时间最长吗？

A: 康熙皇帝，爱新觉罗·玄烨，清朝的第四位皇帝。他在位六十一年。

B: 他给人最深的印象是什么？

A: 他的伟大之处当然是辉煌的文治武功了。他不仅是"康乾盛世"的开拓者，而且是坚定捍卫统一的多民族国家的杰出代表。

B: 原因是什么呢？

A: 我认为有两点非常重要的原因。一是他对国家和历史的责任感。他说："一事不谨，即贻四海之忧；一念不懂，即贻百年之患。"

B: 这位皇帝是以勤政著称的。那第二个原因呢？

A: 二是用人之道。他说过："国家用人，当以德为本，才艺为末。"

B: 我赞同你的看法。不过，我印象最深的是他的读书之道。

A: 看来读书和治国密不可分啊。

生词注解　Notes

① consolidate /kənˈsɒlɪdeɪt/ vt. 巩固；使……固定

② alleviate /əˈliːvɪeɪt/ vt. 减轻；缓和

③ indoctrination /ɪnˌdɑːktrɪˈneɪʃn/　n. 教化；教导

④ environs /ɪnˈvaɪrənz/　n. 政体；社会制度

⑤ seignior /ˈseɪnjə/　n. 领主；藩主

⑥ secession /sɪˈseʃn/　n. 脱离；分离

⑦ annihilate /əˈnaɪəleɪt/　vt. 歼灭；彻底击败

⑧ stipulate /ˈstɪpjuleɪt/　vt. 规定；明确要求

⑨ conducive /kənˈdjuːsɪv/　adj. 有益的；有助于……的

⑩ approach /əˈprəʊtʃ/　n. 方法；途径

第三部分　社稷名流

Part Ⅲ　Distinguished Personages

张骞

Zhang Qian

 导入语　Lead-in

　　张骞(前164～前114)，字子文，汉中郡城固(今陕西城固)人，西汉著名外交家、旅行家和探险家。汉武帝在位时，张骞任郎将侍从，他广交连横，三击匈奴，多次探险西南，开拓云贵川藏。汉武帝因军功封他为博望侯。他不怕艰难险阻，两次出使西域，沟通了中国同西亚和欧洲的通商关系，开拓了历史上著名的丝绸之路，打开了中国与中亚、西亚以及欧洲各国的交往大门，被誉为"东方的哥伦布"。张骞

不仅是中国历史上第一位走出国门的使者,也通过外交实践和阐明了平等互信的外交思想,搭建了国与国之间友好交往的桥梁,促进了国家间的合作与发展。

文化剪影 Cultural Outline

Zhang Qian made two **diplomatic**① missions to the Western Regions. The first lasted for thirteen years from 139 BC to 126 BC, with an aim to unite Darouzhi and attack Xiongnu. When returning to Han, only Zhang Qian and Gan Fu were left among more than one hundred people. The second visit lasted four years, with more than three hundred **retinues**② and myriads of riches; its mission was fulfilled. On one hand, the "Han-West Alliance" came into being and Xiongnu was defeated on end; on the other hand, the economic and cultural exchanges began to move forward, expanding the political influence of the Han Dynasty.

张骞曾两次出使西域。首次出使历时十三年,从前139年到前126年,旨在联合大月氏夹击匈奴。归汉时,一行百余人仅剩张骞和甘父两人。二使西域历时四年,随员三百多,财帛无数,完成使命,一方面形成"汉西联盟",连破匈奴,另一方面促进了经济文化的交流,扩大了汉朝的政治影响。

Zhang Qian was the pioneer of the Silk Road. As the first Chinese going abroad, he opened the door to meet mutual needs between East

Asia and West Asia, connected the old China with the remote West, and promoted mutual commerce and trade development. Zhang Qian was also the **forerunner**③ of the Peaceful Diplomacy. As the first national **envoy**④, he not only laid a solid foundation for the prosperity of the Han Dynasty and for the opening up of the dynasties that followed, but also **injected**⑤ new vitality into the development of world civilization.

张骞是丝绸之路的开拓者。作为第一位走出国门的中国人,他打开了东亚和西亚之间互通有无的大门,连接了古老的中国和遥远的西方,促进了彼此之间的商贸发展。张骞还是和平外交的先行者。作为第一位国家使者,他不仅为汉朝的昌盛以及后来王朝的对外开放奠定了坚实的基础,而且给世界文明的发展注入了新的活力。

Zhang Qian dared to attack Xiongnu three times by following Wei Qing and Li Guang, and during the ten years of detainment in Xiongnu, he could "maintain the integrity of an envoy of the Han Dynasty" all the time, showing his firm determination and fighting spirit. He was a man of great faith. During his first visit to the Western Regions, more than a hundred of his attaches sacrificed their lives for justice. None of them betrayed or escaped. After his second westward journey, the Han envoys were all known as Bowang **Marquis**⑥, Zhang Qin's title. Because of his diplomatic missions to the Western Regions, he opened the Silk Road, bridging economic and cultural exchanges between east and west for the first time.

张骞敢于随卫青、李广三击匈奴;被匈奴拘押十年,他能始终"持汉节不失",彰显出坚定的决心和斗志。他宽大信人,一使西域期间,随员百余人均舍生取义,无一叛逃,二使西域后,汉朝使者皆被西域诸国称为"博望侯"(张骞的封号)。他出使西域,开通了丝绸之路,第一次搭建了东西方的经济文化交流桥。

佳句点睛　Punchlines

1. Zhang Qian remained true to the original **aspiration**⑦ and kept the mission firmly in mind.

张骞不忘初心,牢记使命。

2. Without Zhang Qian's diplomatic missions to the Western Regions, the Silk Road would not have been opened.

没有张骞出使西域,也就不会有丝绸之路的开辟。

3. The Silk Road is a shining road on the past, the present and the **prospect**⑧.

丝绸之路是一条光耀古今、照亮未来的闪光之路。

情景对话　Situational Dialogue

A: Do you know who started the Silk Road?

B: Zhang Qian. He was the first Chinese to have been abroad; it was he who opened the prelude to world history.

A: The Silk Road Economic Belt starts along his Silk Road.

B: Chinese people value that "drinking water, we shouldn't forget the well-digger". So, you want to recall this great veteran. Right?

A: Yes. How can such a great cause be separated from "the first one to have started the world history"?

B: Zhang Qian not only opened up the road to economic prosperity but also carried out the idea of peaceful diplomacy as the first diplomat of China.

A: He inspired future generations: only opening to the outside world can make us more prosperous.

B: Obviously, the great road is not only **inseparable**⑨ from the efforts of modern people, but also from the **legacy**⑩ of ancient people. Only in this way can we carry on the past and live a more exciting life.

A: I think so.

A: 你知道丝绸之路是谁开创的吗？

B: 是张骞。他是中国第一位走出国门的人，是他揭开了世界史的序幕。

A: 丝绸之路经济带就是沿着他开辟的丝绸之路开启的。

B: 中国人讲究"吃水不忘挖井人"，所以你想缅怀一下这位老前辈，是吧？

A: 是的。如此伟大的事业，怎能离得开这位"世界史开幕第一人"？

B: 张骞不仅开创了经济繁荣之路，作为首位中国外交官，他还贯彻了和平外交的思想。

A：他启发后人：只有开放，才能更加繁荣。

B：显然，伟大道路离不开现代人的努力，也离不开古代人的遗产。只有这样，我们才能继往开来，活得更加精彩。

A：我也是这么想的。

生词注解 Notes

① diplomatic /ˌdɪpləˈmætɪk/　*adj.* 外交的；外交上的

② retinue /ˈretɪnjuː/　*n.* 随行人员；扈从

③ forerunner /ˈfɔːrʌnə(r)/　*n.* 先驱

④ envoy /ˈenvɔɪ/　*n.* 使节；（谈判等的）代表

⑤ entourage /ˈɒntʊrɑːʒ/　*n.* （统称）随行人员；随从

⑥ marquis /ˈmɑːkwɪs/　*n.* 侯爵

⑦ aspiration /ˌæspəˈreɪʃn/　*n.* 志向；抱负

⑧ prospect /ˈprɒspekt/　*n.* 前景；前途

⑨ inseparable /ɪnˈseprəbl/　*adj.* 不可分的；不愿分开的

⑩ legacy /ˈleɡəsi/　*n.* 遗赠；遗产

玄奘

Xuanzang

 导入语 Lead-in

玄奘（602~664），本名陈祎，又称"三藏法师""唐僧"，唐朝著名佛学家、翻译家、旅行家，佛相宗创始人。玄奘出身官宦，幼从父学儒家经典，10岁出家洛阳净土寺，16岁入川，师从多师，闻名蜀中，6年后游历各地讲经说法，26岁西行求法，43岁返回长安，一人行程五万里，取得真经，《大唐西域记》详细记述了这段经历，《西游记》也是以其取经事迹为原型。他致力于翻译佛经19年，弘扬佛法，代表译作有《心经》《大般若经》等。

杰出人物

文化剪影 Cultural Outline

Xuanzang devoted himself to Buddhism with great **perseverance**①. He traveled fifty thousand li, went through all the hardships, regardless of life and death, learned **scriptures**② for seventeen years, finally got six hundred and fifty-seven true scriptures, and persisted in translating them for nineteen years.

玄奘献身佛学，矢志不移，行程五万里，历尽艰辛，置生死于不顾，取经十七载，终得真经657部，并坚持译经19年。

Xuanzang's achievements in **Buddhism**③ had a far-reaching influence at home and abroad. In the thirteenth year of his journey to the West, he ever presided over of the Kannauj Buddhist Debate Conference, where anybody was admitted to heckle him but nobody could trouble him and he became famous across the five parts of India for a while, addressed "Heaven of Mahayana" in Mahayana and "Heaven of Liberation" in Hinayana. He insisted on promoting Buddhism, translating seventy-five Buddhist **sutras**④, including one thousand three hundred and thirty-five volumes, which takes up more than half of the total Buddhist translations of the Tang Dynasty, more than doubled the total of other three translators in the history of China while the quality went much beyond that of the **predecessors**⑤ and they became an outstanding model in the history of translation.

玄奘的佛学成就在国内外影响深远。西行第13年,他主持曲女城佛学辩论大会,然而任人诘难,无人成功,一时名震五印,大乘尊称之为"大乘天",小乘尊称之为"解脱天"。他坚持弘扬佛法,共译出75部、含1335卷佛经,超过整个唐朝译经总数的一半,相当于中国历史上另外三大翻译家总数的一倍多,而且质量大大超越前人,成为翻译史上的杰出典范。

The Records of the Western Regions of Great Tang written by Xuanzang was the earliest collection of international news in China as well as in the world, not only the precious literature on the Buddhist history and relics but also the significant information about the history of all the countries in the Central Asia and South Asia, and even precious literature on the research on the transportation between east and west. Smith, a British historian, commented, "The history of the Medieval India was completely dark but he was the only light."

玄奘的《大唐西域记》是中国也是世界上最早的国际新闻集。它不仅是佛教历史和遗迹的重要文献,也是中亚、南亚各国历史的重要资料,甚至是研究东西方交通的珍贵文献。英国史学家史密斯评价:"中世纪印度的历史漆黑一片,他是唯一的亮光。"

佳句点睛 Punchlines

1. In the Chinese history of translating sutras, Xuanzang ended an old era and created a new era.

在中国译经史上,玄奘结束了一个旧时代,开创了一个新时代。

2. The history of the **medieval**⑥ India was in complete darkness, where Xuanzang was the only light.

中世纪印度的历史漆黑一片,玄奘是唯一的亮光。

3. Without the works of Faxian, Xuanzang and Ma Huan, it is entirely impossible to rebuild the history of India.

没有法显、玄奘和马欢的著作,重建印度史是完全不可能的。

情景对话 Situational Dialogue

A: What do you know about Xuanzang?

B: He was surely a Buddhist master.

A: Xuanzang is a really influential Buddhist master and a messenger in cultural exchanges. What can we learn from him then?

B: I think we should first learn from his **dedication**⑦.

A: Dedication goes hand in hand with persistence.

B: We should also learn his great bravery. He had crossed the eight hundred li desert, where there were no birds in the sky or beasts on the ground but vastness around. It is never possible without sacrifice.

A: Xuanzang was one of those who believed in the "unity of knowledge and action" advocated by Wang Shouren of the Ming Dynasty.

B: He was also a man with great patriotism. On his journey to the West, the King of Gaochang tried to **retain**⑧ him and **granted**⑨ him wealth and rank, but he had fasted for three days, persisting in bringing back sutras and returning to the Great Tang.

A: It is the moral integrity.

B: Mr. Lu Xun praised those who sacrificed themselves for the pursuit of truth. Master Xuanzang really deserved it.

A: 你对玄奘有什么了解？

B: 他是一名佛学大师。

A: 玄奘确实是一位有影响的佛学大师和文化交流使者。我们可以从他身上学到什么呢？

B: 我觉得首先要学习他的献身精神。

A: 与献身精神相伴的还有坚持。

B: 我们还要学习他的勇气。他曾横跨八百里沙漠，那里天无飞鸟，地无走兽，四处茫茫。没有牺牲精神，绝不可能做到。

A: 玄奘就是明朝王守仁提倡的那种"知行合一"的人。

B: 此外，他也是一位有伟大爱国情操之人。在他西行途中，高昌国王以荣华富贵极力挽留他，但他绝食三日，坚持取经，回归大唐。

A: 这就是骨气。

B: 鲁迅先生曾赞扬过那些舍身求法的人，玄奘法师真是名至实归。

生词注解 Notes

① perseverance /ˌpɜːsəˈvɪərəns/ *n.* 坚持不懈；不屈不挠

② scripture /ˈskrɪptʃə(r)/ *n.* 圣典；经文

③ Buddhism /ˈbʊdɪzəm/ *n.* 佛教

④ sutra /ˈsuːtrə/ *n.* (佛教或耆那教的)经；箴言

⑤ predecessor /ˈpriːdəsesə(r)/ *n.* 前任；前辈

⑥ medieval /ˌmediˈiːvl/ *adj.* 中世纪的

⑦ dedication /ˌdedɪˈkeɪʃn/ *n.* 奉献；献身

⑧ retain /rɪˈteɪn/ *vt.* 挽留；保留

⑨ grant /ɡrɑːnt/ *vt.* (尤指正式地或法律上)同意；准予

郑和

Zheng He

导入语 Lead-in

郑和(1371~1433),本名马三保,后赐姓郑,又称"三宝太监",云南昆阳州(今昆明)人,明朝著名航海家、外交家。他有智勇,知兵战,通国际风俗。一生七次出使西洋,二十年内跨越半个地球,最大限度远播明朝盛威,梁启超赞其为"航海伟人"。郑和下西洋是一种国家行为,郑和船队是一支强大的战略力量,旨在推行和平外交,稳定东南亚国际秩序,发展海外贸易,传播中华文明。史学家何川文评价说:"自从人类有文明以来,文明之间的交流与交汇,在整个明代的交流与交汇史上,唯有以郑和为代表的中华民族对外交往最文明。"

文化剪影 Cultural Outline

Zheng He made seven voyages to the Western Seas, each with a fleet of over twenty thousand people. On the first voyage, he solved the Java Dispute peacefully and wiped out five thousand pirates. On the second, in a temple of Ceylon he set up a three-language monument to salute to the Buddha, Vishnu and Allah. On the third, in the self-defense war he captured the king of Ceylon. On the fourth, he got to East Africa for the first time; on the voyage back, he captured the **usurper**①. On the fifth, he sent the visiting envoys home as far as to East Africa. On the sixth, he sent the messengers from sixteen countries back home and many other envoys came to China for a tribute. And on the seventh, he made a dragon ship and **mediated**② Siam and Malacca.

郑和七下西洋,每次舰队人数均超两万人。首次出行,和平解决了爪哇争端,剿灭了海盗五千多人。二下西洋,在锡兰的寺庙立三文碑,致敬佛陀、毗湿奴和真主。三下西洋,在自卫战争中生擒锡兰国王。四下西洋,首次到达东非,返航时生擒篡位者。五下西洋,送诸国使者回国,最远到达东非。六下西洋,送返十六国使者,多国使者也来华朝贡。七下西洋,造龙船,劝和暹罗与满剌加。

Zheng He's voyages peaked the development of **Maritime**③ Silk Road, representing China's prominent contribution to the world maritime civilization. His continental routes between Asia and Africa paved the way for the global sailing of the Europeans. When bypassing the Cape of Hope and arrived in the East African coast, Vasco da Gama, a Portuguese **navigator**①, was told that there were Chinese who had been there more than eighty years before, and later Vasco, piloted by the Arabs, successfully arrived in India along Zheng He's shipping line. *Zheng He's* **Nautical**⑤ *Chart* is the earliest navigating map in the world; lots of Zheng He's investigations of the western Pacific Ocean and the Indian Ocean were more than 450 years earlier than the maritime observations by the British "Challenger".

郑和远航让海上丝绸之路的发展达到巅峰,代表了中国对世界海洋文明的卓越贡献。其亚非洲际航线为欧洲人的全球航海铺平了道路;葡萄牙航海家达伽马绕过好望角到达东非海岸时被告知八十多年前曾有中国人到过那里,后来达伽马由阿拉伯人领航,沿郑和航线成功达到了印度。《郑和航海图》是世界最早的航海图集,郑和对西太平洋和印度洋的大量调查比英国"挑战者"海洋考察早四百五十余年。

Zheng He was an impeller of the peaceful diplomacy and an initiator of maritime peace. Zheng He's sailing aimed to establish friendly relationships with the Western Seas and build up a good international environment. Wherever he went, he would warn the **bellicose**⑥ island countries "not to bully the small or insult the weak", stopped violence and controlled chaos to declare the prestige of the Ming Empire, advocated Buddhism and Islam to balance religious conflicts or belief antagonism[1], and enhanced trade and cultural exchanges; while promoting peace and harmony among the countries, it spread the Chinese civilization.

郑和是和平外交的推进者,也是海上和平外交的首创者。郑和远航,目的在于建立和西洋的友好关系,创造良好的国际环境。所到之处,或告诫好斗岛国"不可欺寡,不可凌弱",或止暴制乱、宣示明帝国的声威,或宣扬佛教、伊斯兰教,平衡宗教冲突和信仰对立,加强贸易交往和文化交流。这些举措在促进各国和平和谐的同时,也传播了中华文明。

 佳句点睛　**Punchlines**

1. Zheng He was the impeller of the peaceful diplomacy as well as the initiator of maritime peace.

郑和是和平外交的推进者,也是海上和平外交的首创者。

2. Of the so-called great navigators in the world history, how few can keep abreast of him!

全世界历史上所号称航海伟人,能与并肩者,何其寡也。

3. Zheng He spread the idea of loving peace and good neighborly friendship, which was the spiritual wealth and cultural gene shared by the countries in the region.

郑和传播了热爱和平、睦邻友好的思想，正是地区国家共享的精神财富和文化基因。

情景对话 Situational Dialogue

A: Do you know Zheng He's contribution?

B: Surely. He opened up an intercontinental route to the West.

A: Exactly, it was Zheng He who pushed the Maritime Silk Road to its climax, signifying the coming of the era of global voyage.

B: Why is it said that Zheng He opened up the Maritime Silk Road?

A: Because his seven voyages to the West were large in scale, long in route and great in number, the Maritime Silk Road was not just the road to trade, but also the road to diplomacy.

B: I agree with you.

A: If Zhang Qian's two visits to the Western Regions paved the way for peaceful land diplomacy, Zheng He was the pioneer of the maritime peaceful diplomacy, and a model spreading Chinese civilization.

B: Why this comment?

A: As for it, Premier Li Keqiang said, "(Zheng He) did not pillage, expand or no colonize, but left only the **philanthropic**® and chivalrous deeds that have been praised for centuries."

B: It makes sense, it does. There is no invasion in the genes of

the Chinese nation but peace.

A: 你知道郑和有什么贡献吗?

B: 当然知道,郑和下西洋并且开辟了洲际航线。

A: 确切地说,是郑和把海上丝绸之路推向鼎盛,标志着全球航海时代的到来。

B: 为什么说郑和开辟了海上丝绸之路?

A: 因为郑和七下西洋,规模大、线路长、人数多,所以海上丝路不仅是贸易之路,更多的是外交之路。

B: 我同意你的看法。

A: 如果说张骞两使西域,开辟了陆上和平外交的先河,那么郑和就是海上和平外交的开拓者,而且是中华文明传播典范。

B: 何出此言?

A: 关于这一点,李克强总理说:"(郑和)并没有搞掠夺,也没有搞扩张,更没有搞殖民,留下的是当地传颂了几个世纪的善举和义举。"

B: 言之有理。中华民族的基因里没有侵略,只有和平。

生词注解　Notes

① usurper /juːˈzɜːpə(r)/　*n.* 篡位者;侵占者

② mediate /ˈmiːdɪeɪt/　*vt.* 调解;斡旋

③ maritime /ˈmærɪtaɪm/　*adj.* 海的;海事的

④ navigator /ˈnævɪɡeɪtə(r)/ *n.* 航海家；领航员

⑤ nautical /ˈnɔːtɪkl/ *adj.* 航海的；海上的

⑥ bellicose /ˌhɪərˈɑːftə(r)/ *adj.* 好斗的；好战的

⑦ antagonism /ænˈtæɡənɪzəm/ *n.* 敌对；对抗

⑧ philanthropic /ˌfɪlənˈθrɒpɪk/ *adj.* 乐善好施的；慈善的

郑成功

Zheng Chenggong

导入语 Lead-in

郑成功（1624~1662），本名森，又名福松，字明俨、大木。福建南安人，祖籍河南固始。明末清初军事家，民族英雄。1661年，郑成功率领两万五千名将士，数百艘战船，自金门料罗湾出发，经澎湖，渡海峡，骁勇善战，经过激烈的海战，终于打败荷寇，收复台湾，并大力发展生产，休养生息，受到人民拥戴。

文化剪影 Cultural Outline

Zheng Chenggong insisted that "Taiwan is the land of China". Confronted with invaders, he resolutely pointed out the **indelible**③ truth for Chinese people to recover the lost land and eventually recovered Taiwan.

郑成功坚持"台湾是中国之土地也",面对侵略者,毅然指出中国人收复失地是不可磨灭的真理并最终收复台湾。

Zheng Chenggong's recovery of Taiwan was of great historical significance, namely, that Taiwan belongs to China forever. At the end of the Ming Dynasty, the government was corrupt and the Dutch seized Taiwan. Later, Zheng Chenggong led his army across the strait to defeat the Dutch invaders, ending the thirty-eight years of colonial rule, and Taiwan returned to the embrace of the motherland. Zheng Chenggong defended China's **sovereignty**④ and territorial integrity, **manifesting**⑤ the firm will and fighting spirit of the Chinese nation against foreign aggression.

郑成功收复台湾的历史意义极其重大,即台湾永远属于中国。明末政府腐败,荷兰人占领台湾。后来,郑成功率领大军,横渡海峡,打败荷兰侵略者,结束了其三十八年的殖民统治,宝岛台湾回到了祖国的怀抱。郑成功捍卫了中国主权和领土完整,体现出中华民族反抗外来侵略的坚定意志和斗争精神。

Having driven out the foreign invaders, Zheng Chenggong carried out a series of reforms. Firstly, he abolished all of the colonial institutions and adopted the prefecture-county system. Secondly, he exploited the Treasure Island by carrying out the system of station troops and **reclamation**⑥, putting soldiers on farm work; in the meantime, he encouraged the continental coastal inhabitants cultivating Taiwan's land and helped the Gaoshan people improve their production technology. And thirdly, he vigorously strengthened the maritime economy by trading with Japan, Thailand, Vietnam, the Philippines and other countries to promote the **simultaneous**⑦ economic development of Taiwan and the mainland.

驱逐外夷之后,郑成功进行了一系列改革。首先废除一切殖民体制和机构,采用郡县制。其次开发宝岛,推行屯垦制度,寓兵于农,同时鼓励大陆沿海居民开垦台湾,帮助高山族提高生产技术。第三,大力开发海上经济,与日本、泰国、越南、菲律宾等国通商,推动台湾经济和大陆同步发展。

佳句点睛 Punchlines

1. A son has heard his father teach him to be loyal, but not teach him to betray.

子尝闻父教子以忠,未闻教子以贰。

2. In nourishing your mind, nothing is better than **temperance**⑧;

in pursuing your bliss, nothing is better than reading.

养心莫善寡欲,至乐无如读书。

3. To make our country prosperous, we cannot neglect the oceans.

欲国家富强,不可置海洋于不顾。

 情景对话 Situational Dialogue

A: What person do you think of Zheng Chenggong?

B: He was surely a great hero.

A: Why do you think so?

B: Because he firmly believed that the territory of China cannot be inseparable, he defeated the Dutch invaders and recovered Taiwan.

A: In this case, he was a militarist.

B: Sure. He was also a poet. Listen to a poem he wrote: "Looking up, I see the verdant fairy hills; bending down, my eyes fall on the yellow cauliflowers. The billowing waves refreshes me; the breeze from pine trees is blowing my clothes."

A: Wow, Zheng Chenggong was simply a fantasticly typical lyric poet.

B: He was an **intellectual**® general.

A: If he had not died young, he could have written more masterpieces.

B: Definitely. Nevertheless, he would surely shine in the history of Chinese civilization anyway.

A: Yes. He would go down in history forever that he safeguarded the territorial integrity of the motherland and saved people from the abyss of suffering.

A：你认为郑成功是一位什么样的人？

B：他当然是一位大英雄了。

A：何以见得？

B：他坚信中国领土不可分割，打败荷兰侵略者，收复台湾。

A：这么说，他还是一位军事家。

B：当然。他还是一位诗人。听我给你念一首他写的诗："仰看仙岑碧，俯首菜花黄。涛声怡我情，松风吹我裳。"

A：哇，郑成功竟有这等手笔，简直是典型的抒情诗人。

B：是啊，人家可是儒将呢。

A：要不是英年早逝，他肯定能写出更多的佳作。

B：肯定能。不过郑成功终将在中国文明史上大放光彩。

A：是的，他捍卫祖国领土完整，救民于水火，终将永载史册。

生词注解 Notes

① stalemate /ˈsteɪlmeɪt/ n. 相持；僵持局面

② overawe /ˌəʊvərˈɔː/ vt. 使……极为敬畏；使……胆怯

③ indelible /ɪnˈdeləbl/ adj. 不可磨灭的；无法忘记的

④ sovereignty /ˈsɒvrəntɪ/ n. 主权；最高权威

⑤ manifest /ˈmænɪfest/ vt. 表明;清楚显示(尤指情感、态度或品质)

⑥ reclamation /ˌrekləˈmeɪʃn/ n. 开垦

⑦ simultaneous /ˌsɪmlˈteɪnɪəs/ adj. 同时的;同时发生的

⑧ temperance /ˈtempərəns/ n. 节制;节欲

⑨ intellectual /ˌɪntəˈlektʃuəl/ adj. 有高智力的

林则徐

Lin Zexu

林则徐（1785～1850），字元抚，又字少穆、石麟，晚号俟村老人、俟村退叟、七十二峰退叟、瓶泉居士、栎社散人等，福建侯官（今福州）人。清朝卓越的政治家、思想家和诗人。出身贫寒，幼受父亲启蒙，少读鳌峰书院，师从郑光策。两次落第，二十六岁起从政。因虎门销烟广东抗英而成一代名臣，又因鸦片战争而成为"罪臣"，被流放四年。晚年先后经略陕甘、云贵、广西、广东等地。林则徐是中国引进国际法的鼻祖、中国近代外交事业的先锋和中国国际法学的开创者，他还是中国近代史上一位伟大的爱国者和杰出的民族英雄。

文化剪影 Cultural Outline

Lin Zexu was poor in boyhood, but he was diligent, **studious**① and ambitious. In politics for thirty-six years and in thirteen provinces, he stuck to his high **aspiration**② by guarding sovereignty and territory and developing national industry and commerce; he would often "put **weal**③ or woe and honor or disgrace beyond measure", and even in exile he wrote, "Were it to benefit my country I would lay down my life; what then is risk to me"? Lin Zexu was a model of constant self-improvement and moral excellence.

林则徐少小家贫,但勤奋好学,有雄心壮志。他从政三十六年,历经十三省,坚持高远之志,捍卫主权领土、发展民族工商业,常"置祸福荣辱于度外",即使流放期间,仍不忘忧国忧民,曾写下"苟利国家生死以,岂因祸福避趋之"。林则徐堪称自强不息、厚德载物的典范。

Lin Zexu was a great hero in the modern history of China. He led the nineteen-month anti-opium campaign represented by the Humen Destroying Opium, declaring to the whole world the determination of the Chinese nation not to yield to **aggression**④; he defeated the western armed aggression represented by Britain many times, turning the brilliant first page in the anti-imperialism in the modern history of China. His heroic feat of the opium-banning campaign defended national interests and national dignity and increased the aspirations of the Chinese people.

林则徐是中国近代史上一位民族大英雄,领导了以虎门销烟为代表、为期十九个月的禁烟运动,向全世界宣告了中华民族不屈服于侵略的决心,多次打败以英国为代表的西方武装侵略,翻开了中国近代史上反帝斗争中光辉的第一页。林则徐领导禁烟运动的英雄壮举,维护了国家利益和民族尊严,增长了中国人民的志气。

Lin Zexu was the first "to watch the world with an open eye". The Opium War made him see his countrymen's ignorance of the outside world, so he set up a team to translate western newspapers and magazines. He was inspired by western translation to "control foreigners by learning their advantages". The translation of *Four Continents' Records*, i.e. *The Encyclopedia of the World Geography*, introduced the history, geography and politics of the various countries in the world more **systematically**[⑤]. *International Law* not only met the needs to struggle against the enemy and diplomacy but also was an epoch-making event, marking the formal spreading of the western international law into China and the beginning of the science of international law in China.

林则徐是近代中国"开眼看世界"的第一人。鸦片战争让他看到国人对外部世界的无知,于是他组建队伍,翻译西方报刊杂志。西学翻译让他萌生"师夷长技以制夷"的思想。译著《四洲志》,即《世界地理大全》,较为系统地介绍了世界各国的历史、地理、政治等情况;译著《国际法》,不仅满足了当时对敌斗争和外交的需要,而且是一件划时代的大事,标志着西方国际法正式传入中国,也标志着中国国际法学的开端。

佳句点睛　Punchlines

1. An official should first make body and mind upright; and there are peerless exploits in public praise.

为官首要心身正,盖世功勋有口碑。

2. It is not as we would like it, but keep it clear of our heart.

岂能尽如人意,但求无愧我心。

3. If my **descendants**^⑥ are as good as I, what use with money? When they're wise, it will harm their aspirations. When they're not, what use with money? When they're foolish, it will increase their faults.

子孙若如我,留钱做什么,贤而多财,则损其志;子孙不如我,留钱做什么,愚而多财,益增其过。

情景对话　Situational Dialogue

A: In modern China, there is one figure, known as a great national hero. Do you know?

B: Definitely Lin Zexu. He was world-famous for waging the Opium-banning Movement.

A: It was for the Movement that the British Empire launched the disgraceful Opium War.

B: In that case, Lin Zexu was a worthy national hero against invasion.

A: Right. Bear in mind, the war started with the greedy British imperialism. In order to **safeguard**⑦ national interests and national dignity, the Chinese people were forced to get involved into the war. Due to his courage, forethought and determination, Lin won a series of victories against the imperialism.

B: What is worth praising was not just his feats fighting against foreign invasion.

A: You might as well state out.

B: The first is his thought of "saving the world through economy". Wherever he went, he was always down-to-earth; even in exile, he did not forget to **benefit**⑧ the people.

A: It's worth of learning. What's the other one?

B: The other is his idea that "to be an official is to first make body and mind upright".

A: Honest and upright officials are always welcome by the common people.

A: 近代中国有一位人物,被誉为一位伟大的民族英雄。你知道吗?

B: 肯定是林则徐了。他因领导了禁烟运动而闻名世界。

A: 正是由于这场运动,大英帝国发动了可耻的鸦片战争。

B: 如此说来,林则徐不愧为抵御侵略的民族英雄。

A: 对。要牢记,这场战争始于贪婪的大英帝国主义。为了捍卫民族利益和民族尊严,中国人民被迫卷入了这场战争。林则徐凭借勇气、远见和果断,取得了一系列反帝胜利。

B: 值得称道的不仅仅是他反抗外来侵略的战斗功勋。

A: 不妨直言。

B: 首先是他的"经国济世"思想。无论到哪里,他总是踏实肯干;即使处于流放期间也不忘造福人民。

A: 确实值得学习。还有呢?

B: 其次是他的为官之道——"为官首要心身正"。

A: 正直清廉的官员总是受到老百姓的欢迎。

生词注解 Notes

① studious /ˈstjuːdɪəs/ *adj.* 好学的;用功的

② aspiration /ˌæspəˈreɪʃn/ *adj.* 志向;抱负

③ weal /wiːl/ *n.* 福利;幸福

④ aggression /əˈgreʃn/ *n.* 侵略;侵犯

⑤ systematically /ˌsɪstəˈmætɪklɪ/ *adv.* 系统地;按部就班地

⑥ descendant /dɪˈsendənt/ *n.* 后裔;后代

⑦ safeguard /ˈseɪfgɑːd/ *vt.* 保卫;保护

⑧ benefit /ˈbenɪfɪt/ *vt.* 有益于……;对……有益

第四部分 科技英才

Part IV　Scientific Geniuses

蔡伦

Cai Lun

导入语 Lead-in

蔡伦(？～121)，字敬仲，东汉桂阳郡(今湖南郴州)人。中国古代发明家。蔡伦生于铁匠世家，自幼钟情发明制造，少时便满腹经纶。蔡伦总结以往人们的造纸经验，革新造纸工艺，制成了"蔡侯纸"。汉和帝下令推广他的造纸法。蔡伦的造纸术是中国古代四大发明之一，对人类文化的传播和世界文明的进步做出了重要的贡献，被誉为造纸鼻祖和"纸神"。

文化剪影　Cultural Outline

Cai Lun had preference for invention and manufacturing since childhood. Owing to his help to Emperor He of Han, he was **nominated**① as Shang Fang Ling in charge of the royal manufacturing; he since began to reveal his gifts in engineering technology. He collected all the skilled craftsmen under the heaven and improved production process. He also bettered paper making technology, praised by the emperor and **popularized**② across the country. Nine years later he was promoted as "Marquis Longting" and his invention was called "Marquis Cai Paper".

蔡伦自幼钟情发明制造。因帮助汉和帝收归皇权,被任命为尚方令,负责皇宫制造业,从此开始展现其工程技术方面的天资。他汇聚天下能工巧匠,改善制作工艺。他还继往开来,改进造纸术,得到了皇帝的常识并下令全国推广。九年后,蔡伦官封"龙亭侯",其发明被称为"蔡侯纸"。

Since his charge of Shang Fang Bureau, Cai Lun has got constant inventions, of which the most far-reaching influence was nothing better than his papermaking technology, which is still one cultural card that China reveals to the world up to now. Cai Lun himself was selected into *The List of 100 People Who Have Influenced the Course of Human History*, ranking the sixth.

掌管尚方局以来,蔡伦发明创造不断,个中影响最深远者莫过于其造纸术,迄今依然是中国向世界展示的一张文化名片。蔡伦本人也因此入选《影响人类历史进程的一百人排行榜》,名列第六。

Since ancient times, books were largely compiled with bamboo slips and the silk or cloth used for writing was called "paper". But silks and satins were too expensive to **facilitate**③ cultural **transmission**④ and bamboo slips were too heavy to carry. In combination with the experience of predecessors, Cai Lun selected bark, **hemp**⑤ slices, rags and broken fishing nets as raw materials; after a series of processes and several rounds of experiments, he eventually invented the tough Marquis Cai Paper. Its most distinctive feature is that it is wide-ranging in materials, low in price and easy to carry, completely avoiding the disadvantages of bamboo slip books and silk books, and more **conducive**⑥ to the inheritance and **diffusion**⑦ of knowledge and culture. Cai Lun was "a great Chinese inventor who changed the face of world culture".

自古书籍多用竹简编成,写字的绸缎、布匹被称为"纸张"。然而绸缎太贵,不方便文化传播,竹简太重,不利于运送。蔡伦结合前人经验,选取树皮、麻片、碎布头、破渔网为原料,经过一系列工艺,几经试验,终于发明了韧性十足的"蔡侯纸"。其最大特色是取材广泛、价格低廉、便于携带,完全避免了简书和帛书的弊端,更有利于知识文化的传承传播。蔡伦也被称为"一位改变世界文明面貌的中国伟大的发明家"。

 佳句点睛　Punchlines

1. The opening ceremony of the 2008 Beijing Olympic Games featured the papermaking technique invented by Cai Lun.

2008年北京奥运会开幕式上,特别展示了蔡伦发明的造纸术。

2. Without paper, what will happen to the world?

没有纸,世界将会怎样?

3. Cai Lun's paper-making technique spread to the whole world through Central Asia and Western Europe along the Silk Road, making **indelible**® contributions to the inheritance and development of world civilization.

蔡伦的造纸术沿着丝绸之路经过中亚、西欧向整个世界传播,为世界文明的传承与发展做出了难以磨灭的贡献。

 情景对话　Situational Dialogue

A: What will the world be without paper?

B: Without paper, there would be neither Wang Xizhi's *Sketch to the Gathering at Orchid Arbor* in the East nor Shakespeare's *Hamlet* in the West. Without paper, we may know nothing about the world. Where do we read human history and where do we write history?

A: Then, who contributes the most to papermaking?

B: Cai Lun. It's he who invented Marquis Cai Paper that greatly improved papermaking.

A: Cai Lun is also said that "the first great Chinese inventor who changed the face of world culture".

B: It stands to reason. It is he who made paper fly into each common household. People all over the world, have got more chances to read.

A: Cai Lun was really great, for he promoted civilization by benefiting the common people.

A: 没有纸,世界会是什么样?

B: 没有纸,东方会没有王羲之的《兰亭集序》,西方也不会有莎士比亚的《哈姆雷特》。没有纸,我们可能会对世界一无所知。我们在哪里阅读世界,在哪里书写历史呢?

A: 谁对造纸术的贡献最大呢?

B: 蔡伦。正是他发明的"蔡侯纸"推动了造纸术的发展。

A: 还有人评价蔡伦是"一位改变世界文明面貌的中国伟大的发明家"。

B: 言之有理。是他让纸"飞入寻常百姓家"的。让世界各地的人们有了更多的读书机会。

A: 蔡伦真伟大,他通过造福百姓而推动了文明发展。

生词注解 Notes

① nominate /ˈnɒmɪneɪt/ vt. 任命；提名

② popularize /ˈpɒpjələraɪz/ vt. 推广；普及

③ facilitate /fəˈsɪlɪteɪt/ vt. 促进；使……便利

④ transmission /trænsˈmɪʃn/ n. 传播；传输

⑤ hemp /hemp/ n. 麻类植物；大麻

⑥ conducive /kənˈdjuːsɪv/ adj. （对某事）有助益的；使……容易发生的

⑦ diffusion /dɪˈfjuːʒn/ n. 传播；扩散

⑧ indelible /ɪnˈdeləbl/ adj. 不可磨灭的

李时珍

Li Shizhen

导入语　Lead-in

李时珍(1518～1593),字东壁,晚号濒湖山人,明朝蕲州(今湖北蕲春)人。中国古代著名医学家、药物学家,后世尊其为"药圣"。李时珍生于医学世家,二十三岁随父学医,闻名乡里。三十三岁治好富顺王之子,声名鹊起,被聘为楚王府奉祠正,三十八岁入京任太医院判,四十二岁辞官,经营东璧堂,从事药物研究,历经三十八年,三易其稿,于1590年完成了巨著《本草纲目》。李时珍打破了《神农本草经》以来沿袭了一千多年的上、中、下三品分类法,把药物分为水、火、土、金石、草、谷等十六部,包括六十类,系统记述了各种药物的知识,极大丰富了本

草学的知识。此外,他对脉学及奇经八脉也颇有研究,著有《奇经八脉考》《濒湖脉学》等。

 文化剪影 Cultural Outline

Li Shizhen was fond of herbal medicine as a boy. Employed with the Imperial Academy of Medicine, he was mainly occupied in research on herbal medicine, reading through the precious books stored in the royal collection and collecting plenty of writing materials. Four years later he resigned to his hometown and set up Dongbitang, serving the people to gain plentiful clinical experiences and studying herbal medicine. In his prime he travalled through the famous mountains and great valleys, examined the characteristics of medicinal herbs, **clarified**[①] their names, interviewed extensively, gathered various recipes and completed *The* **Compendium**[②] *of Materia Medica*.

李时珍自幼钟情本草。任职太医院期间,主要从事本草研究,他饱览皇家珍藏,搜集众多创作素材。四年后,李时珍辞官返乡,创立东壁堂,一面服务百姓,获得大量临床经验,一面研究药物。他在壮年时期,走遍名山大川,考究药草习性,厘清药草命名,同时广泛采访,搜罗百方,完成了《本草纲目》。

Li Shizhen had *Research on Eight Extra-Meridian Channels, Binhu Study on Pulses* and *The Compendium of Materia Medica* in existence. Based on past literature, the first detailed the circulation of the eight extra-meridian channels, attached with his opinions. The second briefed twenty-seven pulse conditions logically and readably, spread quite **extensively**③, deserving a model of Chinese medicine. And the final was widely believed to be his most famous masterpiece.

李时珍的现存著作有《奇经八脉考》《濒湖脉学》和《本草纲目》。第一本基于历代文献,对奇经运行详加说明,并附个人见解。第二本归纳二十七种脉象,语言简明,论述逻辑,朗朗上口,流传很广,堪为中医典范。最后一本被普遍认为是其最负盛名的杰作。

Research on Eight Extra-Meridian Channels developed the meridian-**collateral**④ theory and *Binhu Study on Pulses* improved the establishment of Chinese medicinal theory, while *The Compendium of Materia Medica* has been regarded as the greatest scientific achievement of the Ming Dynasty. The grand work not only went through as long as forty-three years, when Li Shizhen's disciples and sons made great contributions to its **compilation**⑤ and publication, but also reflected his **distinctive**⑥ academic ideas and research methodology, which made the far-reaching influence on the world medicine, botany, zoology and chemistry.

《奇经八脉考》发展了经络学说,《濒湖脉学》促进了中医理论的建立,而《本草纲目》则被认为是明代最伟大的科学成就。这部鸿篇巨著历时四十三年完成,期间李时珍的弟子和儿子们对它的编纂和出版均有巨大的贡献,该书还体现出李时珍富有特色的学术思想和研究方法,在世界医药学、植物学、动物学、化学方面具有深远的

影响。

佳句点睛　Punchlines

1. Medicine is "fit to treat an illness but not to take as food".
药物"治病可也,服食不可也"。

2. Li Shizhen was a famous medical scientist in the Ming Dynasty, honored as the "Medical Saint" by later generations.
李时珍是明代著名医学家,被后世誉为"医圣"。

3. *The Compendium of Materia Medica* had been the most systematic, complete and scientific pharmacologic work in China till sixteenth century.
《本草纲目》是十六世纪为止中国最系统、最完整、最科学的一部医药学著作。

情景对话　Situational Dialogue

A: What kind of person was Li Shizhen?

B: He was a great medical scientist, who wrote a great book, entitled *The Compendium of Materia Medica*. But I'm more interested in his *Research on Eight Extra-Meridian Channels*.

A: Why? The former is his masterpiece.

B: Because I like Taijiquan, and one of its fundamental theories is the subject of channel and collateral, mainly about the eight extra-meridian channels.

A: I'm a literature lover so I'm more concerned with his story. I discover that a famous doctor can not only save the living from death but also diagnose them to death.

B: Why do you utter such things?

A: One day, Li Shizhen came across a group of mourners, saying a pregnant woman died. Having persuaded her family, Li Shizhen massaged her for a while and then put a needle into her chest. Can you guess what happened? The woman survived and soon gave birth to a **chubby**⑦ baby boy.

B: A real miracle.

A: In fact, nothing miraculous. Li Shizhen discovered her blood was fresh rather than **clotted**⑧.

B: What do you mean by predicting a person to be dead?

A: A store owner's son jumped over the counter after a meal. Li Shizen happened to pass by and walked up to take his pulse. He said the son could only live for six hours, so he was fiercely cursed. However, six hours later the son died of overeating, for the sudden jump broke his **intestines**⑨ and severely injured his internal organs.

B: It's really amazing that Li Shizhen could predict the development of an illness.

杰出人物

A: 李时珍是位什么样的人物?

B: 他有一部巨著,叫《本草纲目》。不过,我更感兴趣的是他的《奇经八脉考》。

A: 为什么?《本草纲目》可是他的代表作。

B: 因为我喜欢太极拳,而太极拳的基础理论之一就是经络学说,主要就是"奇经八脉"。

A: 我是个文学爱好者,所以我更关注他身上的故事。我发现,名医就是不仅能把将死之人治好,还能替"活人断死"。

B: 何出此言?

A: 有一天,李时珍碰上一群送殡的人,说是死了一个孕妇。李时珍说服其家人,一番按摩,往孕妇胸口扎了一针。你猜怎么样?孕妇活过来了,不久还生了个大胖小子。

B: 真是奇迹。

A: 其实也没什么稀奇。李时珍发现孕妇的血是鲜血,而非淤血。

B: 那你说的"活人断死"是怎么回事?

A: 一个店老板的儿子饭后翻越柜台。恰好李时珍路过,上前一把脉,说他只有三个时辰的阳寿,结果被人家大骂一顿。可是,三个时辰后,这人真死了。原来,病人吃饭过饱,又翻越柜台,肠子断了,内脏严重受损。

B: 李时珍能预见病情发展,真让人叹为观止。

生词注解 Notes

① clarify /ˈklærəfaɪ/　　vt. 澄清；阐明

② compendium /kəmˈpendɪəm/　　n. 纲要；汇编

③ extensively /ɪkˈstensɪvlɪ/　　adv. 广阔地；广大地

④ collateral /kəˈlætərəl/　　adj. 并行的

⑤ compilation /ˌkɒmpɪˈleɪʃn/　　n. 编辑；汇编

⑥ distinctive /dɪˈstɪŋktɪv/　　adj. 独特的；有特色的

⑦ chubby /ˈtʃʌbɪ/　　adj. 胖乎乎的；圆胖的

⑧ clotted /ˈklɒtɪd/　　adj. 凝结的

⑨ intestine /ɪnˈtestɪn/　　n. 肠；内脏

钱学森

Qian Xuesen

 导入语 Lead-in

钱学森(1911~2009),上海人,祖籍浙江临安。中国伟大的科学家,"两弹一星"元勋,被誉为"中国航天之父"和"中国导弹之父"。十二岁就读北京师范大学附属中学,十八岁就读铁道部交通大学,二十四岁入学麻省理工学院,后转入加州理工学院,师从冯·卡门,二十八岁成为世界知名空气动力学家,先后获航空硕士和航空、数学博士学位,担任麻省理工学院和加州理工学院教授。四十四岁回国,四十八岁入党,贡献卓越。曾获2007年"感动中国"年度人物,"感动中国"组委会的颁奖词这样写道:"在他心里,国为重,家为轻,科学最

重,名利最轻。开创祖国航天,他是先行人,披荆斩棘,把智慧锻造成阶梯,留给后来的攀登者。他是知识的宝藏,是科学的旗帜,是中华民族知识分子的典范。"

文化剪影 Cultural Outline

Qian Xuesen and his mentor Theodore von Kármán completed the research project of high speed **aerodynamics**① and founded "Kármán-Tsien Formula", which is famous all over the world. Within less than half a year, he proposed establishing the **Aviation**② Industry Commission and organized the first Rocket and Missile Research Institute of China; three years later, he proposed to set up the University of Science and Technology of China (USTC), training talents for aerospace. Within fifteen years, he successfully completed the project of *Two Bombs and One Satellite*, creating the world wonders and making the voice of China heard in the field of aerospace.

钱学森和导师冯·卡门完成高速空气动力学研究课题,建立"卡门-钱学森公式",闻名全世界。归国不到半年,钱学森便建议成立航空工业委员会,并组建中国第一个火箭、导弹研究所;三年后,建议成立中国科学技术大学,为航空航天事业培养人才。十五年间,他成功完成了"两弹一星"工程,造就了世界奇迹,在航空航天领域发出了中国声音。

Qian Xuesen is an outstanding representative of patriotic scientists.

The moment he heard that People's Republic of China was founded, he consulted his wife about returning home to offer service. Hardly had he come back when he threw himself into the cause to serve the people. Three years later the USTC was initiated, five years later the first short-range missile was successfully tested, nine years later there was the first atomic bomb and twelve years later the first hydrogen bomb was launched. Three years passed, China had the first man-made satellite, transmitting the melody of *The East Is Red* in the vast space.

钱学森是爱国科学家的杰出代表。刚获悉新中国成立，他便和夫人蒋英商量回国效力。回国后立即投身为人民服务的事业。在他回国的三年后，中国科学技术大学成立；五年后，第一枚近程导弹试验成功；九年后，第一颗原子弹成功爆炸；十二年后，第一颗氢弹成功爆炸；十五年后，中国有了第一颗人造卫星，在茫茫太空播放《东方红》的旋律。

Qian Xuesen wrote a lot and had a great influence. Working in America, he firstly put forward the concept of physical mechanics, explored a new field of high temperature and high pressure, and published *Engineering **Cybernetics***[③], initiatively generalizing cybernetics into engineering field. Having returned to China, he published *Physical Mechanics Lecture Notes*, *An Introduction to Interstellar Navigation* and *On Systems Engineering*. The former reflects his achievements in physical mechanics that he opened up, the middle remains practically significant to today's space exploration and the latter allows systems engineering to **permeate**④ every corner of society.

钱学森著述颇丰,影响巨大。留美期间,他首提物理力学概念,开拓了高温高压新领域,出版了《工程控制论》,首创性地把控制论推广到工程技术领域。归国后,出版了《物理力学讲义》《星际航行概论》和《论系统工程》;前者反映其开创的物理力学成就,中间对当今太空探索仍有现实意义,后者让系统工程渗透到社会各角落。

佳句点睛 Punchlines

1. I have got no time to consider the past; I just consider the future.
我没有时间考虑过去,我只考虑未来。

2. My cause is in China, my accomplishment is in China, and my **destination**⑤ is in China.
我的事业在中国,我的成就在中国,我的归宿在中国。

3. It is often the last key that opens the door.
常常是最后一把钥匙打开了门。

情景对话 Situational Dialogue

A: Talking of Qian Xuesen, there're a lot of titles, such as "Father of Space Technology".

B: And "Father of Missiles" "King of Rockets" and "Father of Automation in China", etc.

A: He was also awarded the medal of "Two Bombs and One Satellite".

B: Though the medal is honorable, many of his stories are more touching.

A: He was a representative of patriotic personages. Wherever he went, he would have a Chinese heart. But what moved me most was his love story.

B: I'd like to lend an ear.

A: He and his wife Jiang Ying delayed their marriage twice for the sake of each other's careers. During the hard times Jiang Ying did all the housework and gave up her singing career, and *Engineering Cybernetics* was thus born.

B: No wonder, talking of the book, Qian Xuesen regarded it as the **crystallization**⑥ of love.

A: In life, Jiang Ying often introduced music to Qian Xuesen and he was also pleased to enjoy such an artistic companion, saying that "my inspiration comes much out of art".

B: What a true model couple! From them I see a perfect combination of art and science.

A: What an admirable fairy companion!

B: Take your hand and grow old with you.

A: 说起钱学森,那可是有说不完的头衔,比如说,"航天之父"。

B: 还有"导弹之父""火箭之王""中国自动化控制之父",等等。

A: 他还被授予了"两弹一星"勋章。

B: 勋章固然可敬,他的故事更加感人。

A: 他是爱国人士的代表,到哪里都有一颗中国心。不过,让我最感动的是他的爱情故事。

B: 说来听听。

A: 他和夫人蒋英为了彼此的事业,两次推迟婚姻。在艰苦的日子里,蒋英包揽家务并放弃歌唱事业,《工程控制论》在这种情况下诞生了。

B: 怪不得,钱学森将这本书视为爱情的结晶。

A: 生活中,蒋英常给钱学森介绍音乐,而钱学森也乐于享受这种艺术熏陶,他说:"我的灵感,许多就是从艺术中悟出来的。"

B: 真是一对模范夫妻。从他们两人身上,我看到了艺术和科学的完美结合。

A: 真是令人羡慕的神仙伴侣啊!

B: 携子之手,与子偕老。

生词注解 Notes

① aerodynamics /ˌeərəʊdaɪˈnæmɪks/ n. 空气动力学;空气动力

② aviation /ˌeɪviˈeɪʃn/ n. 航空;飞机制造业

③ cybernetics /ˌsaɪbəˈnetɪks/ n. 控制论（研究电子机械和人脑工作的一门科学，开发能近似人类思维方式的机器人）

④ permeate /ˈpɜːmieɪt/ vt. 渗透；弥漫

⑤ destination /ˌdestɪˈneɪʃn/ n. 目的地；终点

⑥ crystallization /ˌkrɪstəlaɪˈzeɪʃn/ n. 结晶化；具体化

邓稼先

Deng Jiaxian

 导入语　Lead-in

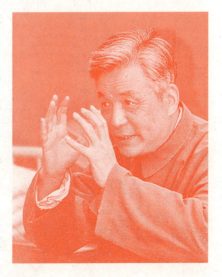

邓稼先(1924~1986)，安徽怀宁人。中国科学院院士，著名核物理学家，"两弹一星"元勋。他领导了爆轰物理、流体力学、状态方程、中子输运等项目，被誉为中国核武器理论研究奠基人。他十七岁考入西南联大，为建设新中国留美就读普渡大学，二十六岁毕业，同年放弃美国优越的科研和生活条件，毅然回国，同王淦昌、彭桓武等创建中国近代物理研究所，开启中国核事业，三十四岁开始领导核武器研究，四十三岁完成两弹工程。作为中国核武器研制工作的开拓者和奠基者，他为中国核武器、原子武器的研

发做出了杰出贡献。他是最具有农民朴实气质的科学家,甘当无名英雄,功勋卓著。

文化剪影 Cultural Outline

Abiding by his father's instruction, Deng Jiaxian devoted himself to learning science to fight against foreign **humiliation**①. After his college years, he worked in Beijing University and threw himself to the struggles for democracy and against **dictatorship**②. Studying in America, he worked hard and took his doctorate within one year and a half, becoming a "baby doctor". After returning to China, he made remarkable achievements; he opened up a new situation in China's nuclear physics research, and then he concealed himself in the vast desert for twenty years and successfully exploded the atomic and hydrogen bombs respectively within nine years, making China's voice heard on the world stage.

邓稼先遵从父亲教导,少年致力于学科学,以抵御外辱。大学毕业,就职于北京大学,投身求民主、反独裁斗争。他留学美国,学习刻苦,一年半便拿到博士学位,成为"娃娃博士"。回国后,成就显著,先是开辟中国核物理研究新局面,后隐身大漠二十年,九年内分别成功研制原子弹和氢弹爆炸,在世界舞台上发出了中国的声音。

Deng Jiaxian was known as "Father of Two Bombs". Together with other heroes of great **distinction**③, he created both the least time to develop the bomb, five years, and the shortest "two bombs interval" in the world, two years plus eight months. Furthermore, the two bombs were born in the American **blockade**④ and the former Soviet Union's isolation, breaking the curse that China could make atomic bombs within 20 years and was typical of "made in China" and "China standards". Deng Jiaxian was also the representative of sharing the common destiny with the motherland. In order to serve the country with science, he used the shortest time to take his doctorate and returned to China. For the sake of national security and world peace, he selected the nuclear cause and took his time in face of its radiation. Deng Jiaxian was a great people's scientist of New China.

邓稼先被誉为"两弹之父"。他和其他元勋一起,既创造了最少的核弹研制时间——五年,又创造了世界上最短的"两弹间差"——两年八个月。不仅如此,两弹还是在美国封锁、前苏联孤立中诞生,打破了"二十年也搞不出原子弹"的诅咒,是典型的"中国制造"和"中国标准"。邓稼先也是与祖国同呼吸、共命运的代表。为了科学报国,他用最短的时间拿到博士学位并归国;为了国家安宁世界和平,他选择了核事业,并从容面对核辐射。邓稼先是新中国伟大的人民科学家。

Deng Jiaxian was a witness and founder of China's nuclear weapons from nonexistence to existence and to excellence. He carried out theoretical research on **detonation**⑤ physics, fluid mechanics, state equation and **neutron**⑥ transport, taking the first step to design nuclear weapons on Chinese own. He took part in the development and tests of the two bombs and went to the frontline to collect data. Ignoring the cancer, he returned to the base to install detonators, but ordered the other people to **evacuate**⑦, on the grounds that "you're still young". He raced against time to push China's nuclear tests to the highest level in the world today. At the last moment of his life, he said, "I still choose China and the nuclear cause."

邓稼先是中国核武器从无到有到优的见证人和缔造者。他开展爆轰物理、流体力学、状态方程和中子输运等理论研究,迈出中国独立设计核武器的第一步。他参与中国两弹的研制和试验,并亲临第一线搜集数据。他不顾癌症在身,回基地装雷管并命令人员撤离,理由是"你们还年轻"。他争分夺秒,把中国核试验推进到当今世界最高水平。在生命的最后,他说:"我仍然选择中国,选择核事业。"

佳句点睛　Punchlines

1. I have known there would be such a day, but I did not expect it comes so soon.

我早就知道有这样一天,只是没想到它来得这么快。

2. Neither for fame nor for profit, but my goal of the work should be at the world's advanced level.

一不为名,二不为利,但工作目标要奔世界先进水平。

3. I don't love weapons and I love peace, but for the sake of peace, we need weapons. If life can **regenerate**⑧, I still choose China and choose the nuclear cause.

我不爱武器，我爱和平，但为了和平，我们需要武器。假如生命终结后可以再生，那么我仍然选择中国，选择核事业。

 情景对话　**Situational Dialogue**

A: Do you know Deng Jiaxian?

B: Yes. He was a man who counted every minute and second and deeply understood that "time waits for no man". For example, he created the "Chinese Speed" to complete the "Two Bombs Project" within just two years plus eight months.

A: I agree with you. With time to spare, he and his team created the world's fastest speed, far faster than the superpowers of the day.

B: He was also a man **indifferent**⑨ to fame and wealth. In his mind, there was only the ambition of serving the country and the people, but no sense of fame and wealth. So he went back to China after graduation and devoted himself to nuclear cause for national security and people's well-being for twenty years of **obscurity**⑩.

A: The old man's last word to his wife was that if life could be reborn, he would still choose China and the nuclear cause.

B: Deng Jiaxian is really a model of not forgetting his original aspiration and sacrificing himself to serve the country.

A: He deserved to be praised "a great life and a glorious death".

B: Right. He was a man who moved China and will always be remembered by the People's Republic of China.

A: 你知道邓稼先吗？

B: 知道。他是一位分秒必争的人，深知"时不我待"。比如，他创造了"中国速度"，仅用两年八个月就完成了"两弹工程"。

A: 我同意。因为惜时如金，他和团队创造了世界最快速度，远超当时的超级大国。

B: 他还是一位淡泊名利的人。他的脑海里只有为国为民之志，没有名利之心。所以他毕业即回国，为国家安全和人民安康致力于核事业，默默无闻二十年。

A: 邓老留给老伴的最后一句话是：假如生命可以重生，他会依然选择中国，选择核事业。

B: 邓稼先真是不忘初心、舍身报国的典范啊。

A: 邓稼先不愧是"生的伟大，死的光荣"。

B: 对。他是一个感动中国的人，是一个永远被中华人民共和国铭记的人。

生词注解　Notes

① humiliation /hjuːˌmɪlɪˈeɪʃn/　n. 蒙羞；耻辱

② dictatorship /ˌdɪkˈteɪtəʃɪp/　n. 专政；独裁权

③ distinction /dɪˈstɪŋkʃn/　n. 卓越；特质

④ blockade /blɒˈkeɪd/ *n.* 封锁；包围
⑤ detonation /ˌdetəˈneɪʃn/ *n.* 爆轰；引爆
⑥ neutron /ˈnjuːtrɒn/ *n.* 中子
⑦ evacuate /ɪˈvækjueɪt/ *v.* 疏散；撤退
⑧ regenerate /rɪˈdʒenəreɪt/ *vt.* 振兴；复兴
⑨ indifferent /ɪnˈdɪfrənt/ *adj.* 漠不关心的
⑩ obscurity /əbˈskjʊərəti/ *n.* 鲜为人知的状态

华罗庚

Hua Luogeng

 导入语 Lead-in

华罗庚(1910~1985),江苏常州人。当代著名数学家,中国解析数论、矩阵几何学、典型群、自守函数论与多元复变函数论等研究领域的创始人和开拓者,中国现代数学之父。十五岁因贫辍学,五年时间自学完高中、大学数学课程。二十岁得熊庆来赏识进入清华大学,自学英、法、德、日四门语言。二十五岁受数学家诺伯特·维纳推荐,次年就读英国剑桥大学,师从哈代。二十七岁学成归国,先后任教清华大学、西南联大和美伊利诺伊大学。四十岁毅然放弃国外优厚待遇,举家归国效力,成果不断,享誉世界,国际上以华氏命名的数学科研成果有"华氏定理""华氏不等式""华-王方法"等。

文化剪影 Cultural Outline

Hua Luogeng studied by himself all the senior high school and college math courses in poverty. He published papers and made a sensation in the math field. He learned four foreign languages on his own at Tsinghua University, and wrote at least fifteen papers within two years at Cambridge University, one of which earned him world reputation. During the Anti-Japan War, he published more than twenty papers and finished his first math **monograph**① *The **Additive**② Prime Number Theory*. He taught in America during the Liberation War. Returning to China, he led the Math Institute of the Chinese Academy of Sciences, attended the first World Congress of Mathematicians after the World War Ⅱ, won first prize of the first State Natural Science Awards and was a leader in Chinese mathematics.

华罗庚在贫困中自学完成高中、大学数学课程。他发表的论文轰动了数学界。他在清华大学自学了四门外语,在剑桥大学两年期间完成了至少十五篇论文,其中一篇为让他响誉世界。抗战期间,他在三年内发表二十多篇论文,完成了第一部数学专著《堆垒素数论》。解放战争期间,他在美国执教。回国后,他领导中科院数学研究所,出席二战后首次世界数学家大会,获得首届国家自然科学奖一等奖,是中国数学界的领路人。

杰出人物

Huo Luogeng is father of China's modern mathematics, opening up analytic number theory, **rectangle**③ geometry, classical group, multicomplex function theory and defensive function theory. He published over 150 academic papers, which have left such mathematic terms as Hua's **Theorem**④, Hua's Inequation and Hua-Wang Method, and of which *The Multicomplex Function Theory over a Typical Domain* won first prize of the first State Natural Science Awards. Besides, there are more than 10 popular science works.

华罗庚是中国现代数学之父,开创了解析数论、矩形几何学、典型群、多复变函数论和自守函数论。他发表的学术论文有一百五十多篇,在国际上留下了"华氏定理""华氏不等式""华-王方法"等数学术语,其中《典型域上的多元复变函数论》获得了国家自然科学一等奖。此外,他还有十多部科普著作。

Hua Luogeng devoted himself to learning, founding and advancing the research in analytic number theory, rectangle geometry, classical group and defensive function theory, over ten years ahead of the world levels. He applied his own theories to practice. He led the team in person to all parts of the country to popularize the **optimum**⑤ seeking method and the overall planning method, which improved workers' efficiency and made great contributions to China's economic development.

华罗庚潜心做学问,开创并推进了中国的解析数论、矩形几何学、典型群和自守函数论等研究,领先世界水平十多年。他把自己提出的理论积极应用于实践,亲自带领团队到全国各地普及优选法和统筹法，提高了工人的工作效率，为中国的经济发展做出了极大贡献。

佳句点睛　Punchlines

1. Grasp what you are interested in, and learn gradually from the simple to the deep.

抓住自己有兴趣的东西，由浅入深，循序渐进地学。

2. Genius lies in accumulation, wisdom in diligence.

天才在于积累，聪明出于勤奋。

3. Learning and research is like climbing a ladder, which needs to climb step by step. If you try to reach the sky by four or five steps at a time, you will surely fall.

学习和研究好比爬梯子，要一步一步地往上爬，企图一脚跨上四五步，平地登天，那就必然会摔跤了。

情景对话　Situational Dialogue

A: Have you ever heard about Hua Luogeng?

B: Of course. When I was in middle school, my teacher told me the story of his **perseverance**⑥ and self-study.

A: What impressed you most about him?

B: What impressed me most was that he was poor in family but not in aspiration and **handicapped**① physically but not intelligently.

A: What's wrong with physical disability?

B: His left leg was permanently disabled. His battlefield should be the realm of mathematics, so he was more single-minded about it.

A: Oh, I see. He was also a patriot. At the beginning of 1950, he gave up the preferential treatment offered by the University of Illinois and moved back to China with his family, becoming one of the first scientists returning from abroad after the founding of new China. On the way home, he stopped in Hong Kong and wrote the famous open letter.

B: Which open letter?

A: *To All Chinese Students Studying in the United States*, in which he said with great emotion, "Good as Liang Garden is, it's not a long-lived place. Come back home!"

B: It's so admirable. What happened then?

A: Later he lived up to expectations and gave Chinese mathematics a leading position in the West for more than a decade.

B: What a great **patriotic**② mathematician!

A: 你听说过华罗庚吗?

B: 当然。中学时老师就讲过他持之以恒、自学成才的故事。

A: 他给你留下印象最深的是什么?

B: 我印象最深的是他家贫志不贫、身残志坚。

A: 身残是怎么回事?

B: 他左腿终身残疾,但他在数学王国的战场上自由驰骋,所以更加心无旁骛。

A: 噢,我明白了。他还是一位爱国者。1950年初,他放弃了伊利诺伊大学的优厚待遇,举家回国,成为新中国成立后第一批海归科学家。归国途中,他在香港停留,写下了那封著名的公开信。

B: 哪封信?

A:《致中国全体留美学生的公开信》,他在信中十分动情地说:"梁园虽好,非久居之乡,归去来兮。"

B: 这真让人敬仰。后来呢?

A: 后来他不负众望,让中国数学领先西方十多年。

B: 真是一名伟大的爱国数学家!

生词注解　Notes

① monograph /ˈmɒnəɡrɑːf/　*n.* 专著;专题文章

② additive /ˈædətɪv/　*adj.* 累积的;叠加色的

③ rectangle /ˈrektæŋɡl/　*n.* 矩形;长方形

④ theorem /ˈθɪərəm/　*n.* (尤指数学)定理

⑤ optimum /ˈɒptɪməm/　*adj.* 最佳的;最适宜的

⑥ perseverance /ˌpɜːsəˈvɪərəns/　*n.* 毅力;韧性

⑦ handicapped /ˈhændɪkæpt/　*adj.* 残疾的;有生理缺陷的

⑧ patriotic /ˌpeɪtriˈɒtɪk/　*adj.* 爱国的

屠呦呦

Tu Youyou

  导入语 Lead-in

屠呦呦（1930~），浙江宁波人。中国著名科学家，诺贝尔生理学或医学奖、共和国勋章获得者。二十一岁就读于北京大学，专攻生药学。二十五岁就职中医研究院，开启职业生涯。1956年完成半边莲和银柴胡两项生药学研究，有效防治血吸虫病，后系统学习中药，合编《中药炮灸经验集成》。1969年开展抗疟药研究。1972年研制成新型抗疟药，1978年定为青蒿素。主要成就是创制抗疟药——青蒿素和双氢青蒿素。2011年获拉斯克临床医学奖。2015年获诺贝尔生理学或医学奖。2016年获"感动中国"2015年度人物、影响世界华人终身成就奖,入选《时代周刊》2016年度"全球最具影响力人物"。2017年获国家最高科学技术奖。

文化剪影 Cultural Outline

Perhaps it was the experlence of getting **tuberculosis**① as a child that gave her a natural passion for medicine. At college she was deeply in love for herbalism and botany, and she became a professional in traditional Chinese medicine with Chinese Academy of Sciences after graduation. In middle age she led her team to commit to anti-malarial medicine; by going through medical books through the ages, based on more than two thousand prescriptions they compiled *Collections of the Proved Anti-malarial Recipes*, containing six hundred and forty drugs against malaria; and by experimenting over two hundred kinds of them and after over three hundred and eighty failures they eventually made **artemisinin**② which is a good antimalarial medicine. In late years, Tu Youyou has never forgotten her original aspiration, striving for her dream and sticking to the forefront of the battle against malaria.

或许是因为小时候患肺结核的经历,她对医药产生了一种天然的情感。大学期间,她尤其钟情本草学和植物学,毕业后成为中科院一名中医药研究员。中年时期,她带队致力于抗疟药物研究,通览历代医书,基于两千多方药,汇成《抗疟单验方集》,内含六百四十种抗疟药物。通过试验其中两百多种药物,历经三百八十多次失败,终于制成抗疟良药——青蒿素。晚年,屠呦呦不忘初心,为梦想奔波,坚守在抗疟战线最前沿。

In the campaign against **schistosomiasis**[3] in the middle 1950s, Tu Youyou carried out an effective **pharmacognostic**[4] study on Chinese lobelia and starwort. In the early 1969, she accepted the commission to study anti-malarial drugs and extracted qinghaosu from wormwood in 1972. And in 1973 she **synthesized**[5] Dihydroartemisinin, whose ten-time effect was discovered until 1992. She saved millions of lives suffering from malaria throughout the globe and proved the clinical value of the traditional Chinese medicine (TCM) to the world. She moved China and the world by "extracting the essence of the ancient culture, implanting it in the contemporary world and helping human beings through a crisis".

20世纪50年代中期,在抗血吸虫病时,屠呦呦对半边莲和银柴胡开展了有效的生药学研究。1969年初,她接到抗疟药研究使命,并于1972年提取出青蒿素;1973年,她又合成双氢青蒿素,其十倍功效直到1992年才被发现。她挽救了全球数百万遭受疟疾折磨的生命,向世界证明了中医的临床价值。屠呦呦感动了中国,也感动了世界。她"萃取出古老文化的精华,深深植入当代世界,帮人类渡过一劫"。

Against the artemisinin resistance, Tu Youyou proposed effective solutions such as "lengthening drug duration" and "converting **adjuvant**[6] drugs". In addition, she led her team to discover that dihydroartemisinin is particularly effective in treating **lupus erythematosus**[7], expanding the indications for artemisinin.

针对青蒿素的抗药性,屠呦呦提出了"延长用药时间""变换辅助药物"等有效的解决方案,此外,她还带领团队,发现双氢青蒿素对于治疗红斑狼疮效果奇佳,扩大了青蒿素的适应症范围。

佳句点睛　Punchlines

1. Scientific research is not about fame and fortune.
科学研究不是为了争名争利。

2. I like the quiet. It is as quiet as a wormwood. I pursue **stoicism**⑧. It is as stoic as the artemisia flower. I yearn for uprightness. It is as upright as the artemisia stem.
我喜欢宁静,蒿叶一样的宁静。我追求淡泊,蒿花一样的淡泊。我向往正直,蒿茎一样的正直。

3. The discovery of artemisinin is a successful example of the collective exploration of traditional Chinese medicine. This award is an honor for Chinese science and traditional Chinese medicine to the world.
青蒿素的发现是集体发掘中药的成功范例,此次获奖是中国科学事业、中医中药走向世界的一个荣誉。

 情景对话 **Situational Dialogue**

A: What do you admire most about Tu Youyou?

B: I admire her most for being the first Chinese to win the Nobel Prize in Medicine.

A: What I admire her most is that she has ever lived in **obscurity**[9], adhering to the service of the world.

B: That's true. It isn't until eighty-five years old that she has gained the worldwide fame. I'm afraid it would be difficult for her to achieve this if she didn't insist on striving for her ideal.

A: We are all dream-chasers. Tu Youyou is a paragon of the dream-chasers.

B: There is still something more respectable. She said, "Scientific research is not about fame or fortune." So, she has devoted herself to the motherland and the people, and integrated the cause into the needs of the country.

A: Without the mission, she would not have made an outstanding contribution to the fight against schistosomiasis. Without the sprit of serving the people, she would not have discovered artemisinin, which has saved millions of lives.

B: She also has a valuable quality, which is that she never claimed artemisinin as her own, but owed it to the collective, describing its discovery as "a successful example of collective exploration of traditional Chinese medicine".

A: 你最佩服屠呦呦哪一点？

B: 我最佩服她是第一位获得诺贝尔医学奖的中国人。

A: 最让我佩服的是，她一生默默无闻，坚持为天下苍生服务。

B: 此言不假。直到八十五岁，屠呦呦才名满天下。要不是坚持为理想奋斗，恐怕很难有如此成就。

A: 我们都是追梦人，屠呦呦就是追梦人的典范啊。

B: 还有更令人钦佩的呢。她说过："科学研究不是为了争名争利。"所以，她把一生都献给了祖国和人民，把事业融到了国家需要当中。

A: 没有使命担当，她就不会有抗击血吸虫病的杰出贡献；没有为人民服务的精神，她也不会发现可以挽救数百万生灵的青蒿素。

B: 她还有一种宝贵的品质，就是她从未把青蒿素据为己有，而是归功于集体，说其发现是"集体发掘中药的成功范例"。

生词注解 Notes

① tuberculosis /tjuːˌbɜːkjuˈləʊsɪs/ n. 肺结核；结核病

② artemisinin /ˌɑːtɪˈmiːsɪnɪn/ n. 青蒿素（抗疟药）；青蒿提取物

③ schistosomiasis /ˌʃɪstə(ʊ)səˈmaɪəsɪs/ n. 血吸虫病

④ pharmacognostic /ˌfɑːməkɒɡˈnɒstɪk/ adj. 生药学的

⑤ synthesize /ˈsɪnθəsaɪz/ vt. 合成；综合

⑥ adjuvant /ˈædʒʊv(ə)nt/ *adj.* 辅助的

⑦ lupus erythematosus /ˈluːpəs erɪθiːməˈtəʊsʌs/ *n.* 红斑狼疮

⑧ stoicism /ˈstəʊɪsɪzəm/ *n.* 恬淡寡欲；坦然淡定

⑨ obscurity /əbˈskjʊərətɪ/ *n.* 鲜为人知的状态

第五部分 文史巨匠

Part V Great Masters of Literature and History

第五部分 文史巨匠

屈原

Qu Yuan

 导入语 Lead-in

屈原（前340～前278），名平，字原，战国后期楚国丹阳（今湖北宜昌）人。中国古代杰出的政治家、文学家，中国历史上伟大的爱国诗人。少年胸怀大志，文武双全；青年春风得意，要兴楚国；中年政治失意，因遭毁谤而先后流放汉北江南；晚年报国无望，怒投汨罗江。著有《离骚》《天问》《九歌》等杰作，寄托了命运之感和历史之叹，为后来的辞赋创作开了先河。梁启超首推屈原为"中国文学家的老祖宗"。胡乔木评价屈原是"中国浪漫主义文学的奠基人"。毛泽东说："屈原的名字对我们

更为神圣。他不仅是古代的天才歌手,而且是一名伟大的爱国者。"

文化剪影 Cultural Outline

Qu Yuan's works mainly consisted of *The Nine Songs*, *Asking Heaven*, *Sorrow after Departure*, and so on. *The Nine Songs* expressed a strong breath of life through poetic dialogue between humans and gods. *Asking Heaven* asked the Heaven one hundred and seventy-two questions reflecting the writer's views of history and nature. *Sorrow after Departure* focused on the author's personal inner feelings, voiced his **resolution**[①] to keep his own lofty moral **integrity**[②], and was of strong romanticism.

屈原作品主要包括《九歌》《天问》《离骚》等。《九歌》通过人与神的诗歌对话,表现出浓厚的生活气息。《天问》连问苍天172个问题,反映了作者的历史观和自然观。《离骚》注重作者本人的内心情感,表达了自己坚守清高节操的决心,具有强烈的浪漫主义色彩。

Sorrow after Departure was Qu Yuan's masterpiece, the longest lyric poem in the history of ancient Chinese literature, the origin of patriotic poems and that of romantic literature. *Sorrow after Departure* is not only highly praised domestically but also enjoys great popularity internationally. Since the first German version in 1852, there have been French, English, Italian, Russian and Hungarian translations coming out, and even more than one version in the same foreign language.

《离骚》是屈原的代表作,是中国古代文学史上最长的一首抒情诗,是爱国主义诗篇的起点,也是浪漫主义文学的源头。《离骚》不仅在国内备受推崇,在国际上也享有盛誉。自从第一个德文译本1852年问世以来,先后有法、英、意、俄、匈等译本问世,甚至同一种外语译本还不止一个。

Qu Yuan's works were rich in image and magnificent in diction, with reflections on and examinations on the origin of human beings, absolute sincerity and sentimental **attachment**③ to the country and nation, and **indignation**④ and anxiety over the difficulties of people's livelihood. With introducing mythology and legends into his poems, there was a unique positive romantic style coming into being. There were a large number of symbolic techniques and metaphors adopted in the works, where **vanilla**⑤ and beauty were representative of noble and pure character, and evil trees and filthy grass a portrayal of vile and evil characters. Qu Yuan's poems were often long and great works, normal and regular in text structure and **imposing**⑥ and **unbridled**⑦ in vigor.

屈原的作品意象丰富,文辞瑰丽,有对人类起源的思考与追问,有对国家民族的赤诚和眷恋,有对民生多艰的愤慨和忧虑。随着屈原引神话传说入诗,从而形成独树一帜的积极浪漫风格。其作品中大量运用象征手法,香草美人成为高洁品质的代表,恶木秽草成为小人奸佞的写照。屈原诗歌常为长篇巨作,篇章结构规范整齐,气势磅礴,汪洋恣肆。

佳句点睛 Punchlines

1. I sigh long and wipe away my tears; I'm grieved at a life full of woes.

长太息以掩涕兮,哀民生之多艰。

2. For the ideal that I hold dear to my heart, I'd not regret to die nine times.

亦余心之所善兮,虽九死其犹未悔。

3. The road stretches ahead far and long, so I shall search earth and heaven.

路漫漫其修远兮,吾将上下而求索。

情景对话 Situational Dialogue

A: What impresses you most about Qu Yuan's poems?

B: *Sorrow after Departure*.

A: Why?

B: Because in it there are lots of graceful lines inspiring me.

A: Can you tell me?

B: For example, "The road stretches ahead far and long, so I shall search earth and heaven." It shows that one should never lose his heart no matter how hard it is. Looking back on Qu Yuan's life, despite being exiled more than once, Qu Yuan remained dedicated and ready to serve his country and people. That kind of patriotism is something we can always learn from.

A: It's really encouraging, especially for the time being, on the way to our great national renaissance. As dream seekers, we need such positive energy. Can you give another example?

B: Another example, "For the ideal that I hold dear to my heart, I'd not regret to die nine times." It's nothing but the historical version of the romantic spirit of the Long March that the revolutionary ideal is higher than the skies.

A: It reminds me of another poem, "Beheading doesn't matter as long as doctrine is there. Even if you killed Xia Minghan, there would be **successors**[⑧]."

B: What they share is such a romantic feeling.

A: 你对屈原的诗篇印象最深的是什么？

B:《离骚》。

A: 为什么？

B: 因为其中有很多优美的诗句激励着我。

A: 能说一说吗？

B: 比如,"路漫漫其修远兮,吾将上下而求索。"这句诗说的是无论多么艰难,人都不可丧失信心。回顾屈原的一生,尽管被流放多次,但屈原还是保持了他的执着,愿意随时效力于国家和人民。这种爱国情怀值得我们永远学习。

A：的确挺鼓舞人的，尤其是现在，我国正处于民族伟大复兴的时候。作为追梦人，我们需要这种正能量。你能再举个例子吗？

B：再比如，"亦余心之所善兮，虽九死其犹未悔。"这简直是历史版本的长征浪漫主义精神——革命理想高于天。

A：这让我想起了另一首诗歌："砍头不要紧，只要主义真。杀了夏明翰，还有后来人。"

B：这种浪漫情怀是他们的共通之处。

生词注解 Notes

① resolution /ˌrezəˈluːʃn/ n. 决心；决议

② integrity /ɪnˈtegrəti/ n. 正直；廉正

③ attachment /əˈtætʃmənt/ n. 依恋；附件

④ indignation /ˌɪndɪgˈneɪʃn/ n. 愤慨；愤怒

⑤ vanilla /vəˈnɪlə/ n. 香草；香草精

⑥ imposing /ɪmˈpəʊzɪŋ/ adj. 壮观的；仪表堂堂的

⑦ unbridled /ʌnˈbraɪdld/ adj. 不受控制的；不受约束的

⑧ successor /səkˈsesə(r)/ n. 继任者；传人

司马迁

Sima Qian

 导入语　Lead-in

司马迁（前145～前90），字子长，夏阳（今陕西韩城）人。西汉著名史学家、文学家、思想家，被后人尊称为"太史公"和"历史之父"。早年从学孔安国和董仲舒，后"究天人之际，通古今之变，成一家之言"，著《史记》，将历史性、思想性和艺术性完美融合，开创了中国纪传体史学和纪传体文学的先河，为后代文学的发展提供了丰富的营养和强大的动力。

柳宗元认为《史记》"浑然天成，滴水不漏，增一字不容；遣词造句，煞费苦心，减一字不能"。郭沫若称它是"中国的一部古代的史诗"。鲁

伯赞说它是"中国第一部大规模的社会史"。鲁迅赞它是"史家之绝唱,无韵之离骚"。

 文化剪影 Cultural Outline

The Records of the Historian, originally known as The Book of the Court Historian, had been completed for fourteen years. It is China's first general history of **chronicles**①, which recorded the history of three thousand years ranging from the Yellow Emperor to Emperor Wu of Han. The main body of the book was Benji (Biographics of Emperors), Shijia (Aristocratic Families) and Liezhuan (Biographies of Important People).

《史记》历经十四年成书,最初称为"《太史公书》",是中国第一部纪传体通史,记载了上自黄帝下至汉武帝的三千年历史。全书的主体是本纪(皇帝传略)、世家(贵族世家)和列传(传记合集)。

The Records of the Historian was the first **biographical**② general history of China, which was described as "The Swan Song of Historian and the Rhythmless Li Sao". It can be rated as a classic in the historian circle, ranking first among "The Twenty-Four History Books" of China. The moment its "five-style structure" was established, it was followed by various historians competitively; and its recording not to exaggerate beauty and not to hide evil was regarded as a tradition, called "The Spirit of Memoir". It is Sima Qian's Records of the Historian that has made the science of history independent of classics and become an independent discipline in the academic field of China.

《史记》是我国第一部纪传体通史,被称为"史家之绝唱,无韵之离骚",堪称史学界经典,名列中国"二十四史"之首。其"五体结构"一经创立,即被各路史家竞相模仿,其"不虚美不隐恶"的记录被当成传统,被称为"实录精神"。司马迁的《史记》让史学独立于经学之外,成为中国学术领域的一门独立学科。

The Records of the Historian integrated literature into historiography, established the tradition of **historiography**③ literature, and provided the literature of later generations with an endless source of characters as well as a wonderful artistic technique. Sima Qian not only inherited the narrative methods of the pre-Qin literature, but also developed a "mutual cross reference". In addition, he **accumulated**④ valuable experience for future generations in the creation of novels through his various artistic methods. *The Records of the Historian* was a model of biographical literature and ancient prose, providing rich **nutrition**⑤ and powerful **impetus**⑥ for the development of literature for future generations.

《史记》融文学于史学,建立了史学文学的传统,既为后世文学提供了源源不断的人物原型,又奉献了精彩纷呈的艺术手法。司马迁不仅继承了先秦文学的叙事方法,而且发展出"互见法"。此外,他刻画人物的艺术手法多样,为后代小说创作积累了宝贵经验。《史记》是传记文学的典范,古代散文的楷模,为后代文学的发展提供丰富的营

养和强大的动力。

佳句点睛 Punchlines

1. Sima Qian is honored as the "Father of History".

司马迁被誉为"历史之父"。

2. People are doomed to death, either weightier than Mount Tai or lighter than a feather.

人固有一死,或重于泰山,或轻于鸿毛。

3. The best thing is to let matters take their own course; the second is to lead people through benefiting them; the third is to teach people with instructions; the fourth is to make people in order; and the worst is to **compete**⑦ with people.

善者因之,其次利道之,其次教诲之,其次整齐之,最下者与之争。

情景对话 Situational Dialogue

A: Have you got any idea about Sima Qian?

B: Of course. He's the greatest historian in the Western Han. His book *The Records of the Historian* is quite popular.

A: He was also an outstanding writer.

B: He was a thinker as well.

A: Why?

B: Because he further developed Lao Tzu's idea. On the one hand, he kept Lao Tzu's **core**® thought that Tao follows nature; on the other hand, he claimed that Heaven follows nature, which is the people's wishes.

A: Do you know he was also an economist? Because he suggested dif-ferent policies to deal with trade and commerce.

B: Sima Qian knew everything and did deserve admiration.

A: What do you admire him most then?

B: His people-oriented idea. He believed that rulers should keep in mind the wishes of the people.

A: Mao Zedong quoted his statement that "People are doomed to death, either weightier than Mount Tai or lighter than a feather" and put forward the glorious judgment of "Serving the People".

A: 你知道司马迁吗？

B: 他是西汉时期最伟大的历史学家，他的《史记》家喻户晓。

A: 他还是杰出的文学家。

B: 他也是一位思想家。

A: 为什么这么说？

B: 因为他进一步发展了老子的思想。一方面，他保留了老子的核心思想——道法自然；另一方面，他认为天法自然，自然就是人民的愿望。

A: 你知道他也是一位经济学家吗?因为他提出了用不同的政策处理商贸问题。

B: 司马迁无所不通,真让人钦佩。

A: 那你最钦佩他什么呢?

B: 他的民本思想。他认为,统治者应该把人民的愿望放在心上。

A: 毛泽东引用过他的"人固有一死,或重于泰山,或轻于鸿毛",并提出了"为人民服务"的光辉论断。

生词注解 Notes

① chronicle /ˈkrɒnɪkl/　*n.* 编年史;年代记

② biographical /ˌbaɪəˈɡræfɪkl/　*adj.* 传记体的;传记的

③ historiography /hɪˌstɒrɪˈɒɡrəfɪ/　*n.* 历史学;历史编纂学

④ accumulate /əˈkjuːmjəleɪt/　*vt.* 累积;积聚

⑤ nutrition /njuˈtrɪʃn/　*n.* 营养;营养品

⑥ impetus /ˈɪmpɪtəs/　*n.* 原动力;推动力

⑦ compete /kəmˈpiːt/　*vi.* 竞争;争夺

⑧ core /kɔː(r)/　*n.* 核心;要点

⑨ fundamental /ˌfʌndəˈmentl/　*adj.* 基本的;根本的

李白

Li Bai

导入语 Lead-in

李白(701～762),字太白,号青莲居士,是盛唐诗坛一颗璀璨的明星,被誉为"诗仙"。其诗极具代表性,充满了独特的浪漫主义色彩,充分展现了盛唐诗歌的独特魅力,与裴旻的剑舞、张旭的草书并称"唐代三绝"。李白身上既有纵横家"辩才谋天下"的见识,又有道家"道法自然"的修炼,还有儒家"济苍生""安社稷"的入世思想。李白的诗想象丰富、豪迈奔放、清新飘逸、奇妙浪漫、不拘声律,代表作有《静夜思》《行路难》《蜀道难》《将进酒》《梦游天姥吟留别》《黄鹤楼送孟浩然之广陵》等。杜甫评价李白的诗:"笔落惊风雨,诗成泣鬼神。"余光中赞

李白的诗:"酒入豪肠,七分酿成了月光,余下的三分啸成剑气,绣口一吐就半个盛唐。"

文化剪影 Cultural Outline

Throughout his life, Li Bai covered a wide range of well-known mountains and rivers, wrote a large number of poems and left behind *The Collection of Li Taibai*. His poems were rich in literary forms and various in artistic conception, expressing the emotional experience with extremely individual characteristics. His style of poetry is bold and **unrestrained**①, fresh and elegant in **rhetoric**②, which has had a profound **impact**③ on the Chinese literary world.

李白一生广览名山大川,诗作众多,有《李太白集》留世。他的诗歌体裁丰富,意境变化万千,主观色彩强烈,抒发极具个人特色的情感体验。他的诗风格豪迈奔放,语言清新飘逸,对中国文坛影响深远。

Li Bai was the master of masters in the Tang poetry and an important personage in the history of poetry, continuing with the past and opening up the future. Taking it as his own duty to restore the traditions of *The Book of Songs* and *Sorrow after Departure*, seeking a poetic realm like "natural beauty of hibiscus rising out of clear water", he integrated the generous atmosphere of the **flourishing**④ Tang period, added to it his own natural and unstrained individuality and resulted in the summit of the Chinese romantic poetry. His poems had a moral character and were politically aloof, which to some extent represented the literati in the feudal society, who sought freedom and dreams in the mountains, fairyland and drunken state as a last **resort**[⑤].

李白是唐代诗歌的集大成者,是诗歌史上承前启后的重要人物。他以恢复《诗经》《离骚》的传统文风为己任,求"清水出芙蓉,天然去雕饰"之诗境,融盛唐之慷慨气象,添自己潇洒豪纵之个性,在文学上造就了中国浪漫主义诗歌的巅峰。他的诗歌有一种道德品性,在政治上颇为孤傲,一定程度上代表了封建社会的文人墨客,不得已时就在山林、仙境和醉乡里寻求自由和梦想。

Li Bai's poems were of strong subjective color, focusing on the description of heroic spirit and passionate feelings; they often shocked the souls with rising and falling **intonations**[⑥] and rhythmical changes but seldom made a specific and detailed description of objective things. Imagination was everywhere in his poetry; through the **exaggerated**[⑦] imagination of society and nature, fairyland and dreamland, and historical clouds and mists, there came into being an artistic technique of embodying objective in subjective. In his poems there were majestic and powerful images as well as beautiful ones with fresh nature.

李白的诗具有强烈的主观色彩,侧重描写豪迈气概和激昂情怀,常用抑扬顿挫的语调和节奏变换让人受到心灵的震撼,很少对客观事物做具体细致的描述。李白的诗天马行空,通过对社会自然、仙境梦境和历史云烟的夸张想象,形成了用主观体现客观的艺术手法,诗中既有气吞山河的壮美意象,又有清新自然的优美意象。

佳句点睛 Punchlines

1. A time will come to brave the wind and the waves, I'll set my cloud-high sail and cross the seas.

长风破浪会有时,直挂云帆济沧海。

2. Drawing a knife to stop water makes it flow faster, raising a glass to drown sorrows makes it grow heavier.

抽刀断水水更流,举杯消愁愁更愁。

3. Peach Lake is one thousand feet deep, but not so deep as our friendship.

桃花潭水深千尺,不及汪伦送我情。

情景对话 Situational Dialogue

A: Do you know who is the most famous romantic poet in China?

B: Li Bai, Of course. He is honored as Fairy Poet.

A: Can you tell me something about his poems?

B: He composed such a sentence, "Like a drifting cloud you'll float away; with the setting sun I'll part from you."

A: I know. They come from the poem *Farewell to a Friend*.

B: Did you take notice of its **metaphors**®?

A: Yes. There are two metaphors. One is that the mood of the traveler is compared to a drifting cloud; the other is that the feelings of old friends are like the setting sun.

B: Did you notice the images?

A: What do you mean?

B: I mean there're two **incredible**® images, namely, the clouds and the sun. The former implies changes and the latter means **eternity**®.

A: Oh, I see. The one who sets off is like a drifting cloud and the one who sees off is like the setting sun. Whatever happens, the truly deep friendship will never change.

B: In fact, that's one of the typical features of Li Bai's romantic poetry.

A: 你知道谁是中国最著名的浪漫主义诗人吗?

B: 当然是李白了,他被尊称为"诗仙"。

A: 你能给我讲讲他的诗吗?

B: 当然可以。他曾经写过这样一句诗:"浮云游子意,落日故人情。"

A: 我知道,出自《送友人》一诗。

B: 你注意过其中的隐喻了吗?

A: 注意过,诗中有两个隐喻。一个是将行者的心境比作流云,另一个说老朋友的感情像夕阳。

B: 那你注意过它使用的意象了吗?

A: 此话怎讲？

B: 我是说，这里有两个匪夷所思的意象：云朵和太阳。前者暗含变化，后者意味永恒。

A: 噢，我明白了。出行之人如浮云，送行之人像金轮。无论发生什么事，真正深厚的友情是绝不会改变的。

B: 这正是李白浪漫诗歌的典型特征之一。

生词注解 Notes

① unrestrained /ˌʌnrɪˈstreɪnd/ *adj.* 无拘无束的

② rhetoric /ˈretərɪk/ *n.* 华丽的辞藻；修辞学

③ impact /ˈɪmpækt/ *n.* 影响；冲击

④ flourishing /ˈflʌrɪʃɪŋ/ *adj.* 繁荣兴旺的；兴盛的

⑤ resort /rɪˈzɔːt/ *n.* 采用的手段或办法

⑥ intonation /ˌɪntəˈneɪʃn/ *n.* 语调；语音的抑扬

⑦ exaggerated /ɪɡˈzædʒəreɪtɪd/ *adj.* 夸张的；言过其实的

⑧ metaphor /ˈmetəfə(r)/ *n.* 隐喻；比喻说法

⑨ incredible /ɪnˈkredəbl/ *adj.* 难以置信的；不可思议的

⑩ eternity /ɪˈtɜːnəti/ *n.* 永恒；永久

杜甫

Du Fu

导入语　Lead-in

杜甫(712～770),字子美,号少陵野老,祖籍襄阳,河南巩县(今河南巩义)人。唐代伟大的现实主义诗人,被后人誉为"诗圣"。杜甫出身没落世族,自幼好学,七岁能诗,崇儒家仁政,怀报国之志。一生游历丰富,然命运多舛,虽有"致君尧舜上,再使风俗淳"的理想,但少有施仁于民的机会,所以他的诗风沉郁顿挫,描述了安史之乱前后的社会动荡和人民疾苦,反映了忧国忧民的责任担当,具有强烈的纪实性特点,被称为"诗史"。杜甫的诗篇对后世影响深远,代表作有"三吏""三别"《春望》《望岳》等。白居易说:"杜诗贯穿古今,尽工尽善。"

 文化剪影 Cultural Outline

Du Fu **advocated**① Confucian benevolence for the people. In his life, he had experienced a lot of misfortunes, but made extraordinary achievements in poetry. More than one thousand five hundred poems have been handed down to the world; versed in lvshi (eight-line poetry) and ancient-style poetry, he not only refined the rhythm and the language, but also expanded the content and system innovation, which paved the way for the systematic creation of the new yuefu poetic style led by Yuan Zhen and Bai Juyi thereafter. His poetry was an important turning point in the development of the Tang poetry, which had reached the peak of Chinese realistic poetry.

杜甫推崇儒家的仁政为民。他一生辗转多有不幸,但诗文成就不凡,有1500多篇流传于世,以律诗和古体诗见长,不仅韵律齐整、语言精练,而且内容拓展、体制创新,为后来元稹和白居易引领的新乐府诗体创作开辟了道路。杜诗是唐代诗歌发展的一个重要转折点,达到了中国现实主义诗歌的巅峰。

Of all the great Tang poets, Du Fu wrote the most numerous and extensive poems. By leading history into poems, he opened up the new yuefu poetry, and by combining historical authenticity and social broadness, he developed the extensive and profound "Poetic History". Du Fu was also the founder of the art of lvshi poetry; there was a lot of exploration in diction, sentence-making, **antithesis**②, formats and rhymes, and subjects. On one hand, he took full advantage of the **aesthetic**③ specialty of lvshi, whose value was upgraded to the same level as jueju (four-line) and ancient-style poetry; on the other hand, he perfectly integrated his personal concerns about his country and people into the social reality of political **upheavals**④, which opened up a new world for the contents of the metrical poems.

在众星璀璨的唐朝诗人中,杜甫的诗数量最多、内容最广泛。他引史入诗,开创了新乐府诗,融和历史的真实性和现实的广阔性,形成了博大精深的"诗史"。杜甫还是律诗艺术的奠基人,在用字、造句、对仗、格律、题材等方面均有大量探索,一方面充分发挥了律诗的美学特长,将律诗的价值提到与绝句和古体诗相同的高度,另一方面完美融合了个人忧国忧民的情怀和政治动荡的现实,开辟了律诗内容的新天地。

Du Fu's poetry is revered as "Poetic History", giving expression to his inheritance of Sima Qian's spirit of **authentic**⑤ records. He lived through not only the prosperity and splendor of the Kaiyuan Flourishing Age but also the hardships and sufferings for the Rebellion of An Lushan and Shi Shiming. His poems had a distinct realistic writing tendency, reflecting the characteristics of the Tang Dynasty from prosperity to decline. Influenced by the changing times and personal frustrations, the style of his poems was **diversified**⑥, the language profound and forceful, embodying his rich social experience and strong political color.

杜甫的诗被誉为"诗史",体现了司马迁实录精神的传承。他经历过开元盛世的繁华昌盛,也经历过安史之乱的民生疾苦。他的诗有着鲜明的写实倾向,折射出唐王朝由盛转衰的时代特色。受时代变换和个人坎坷的经历影响,他的诗风格多样,语言沉郁顿挫,体现了丰富的社会阅历和强烈的政治色彩。

佳句点睛　Punchlines

1. When you stand on the summit and see, the mountains around and below are wee.

会当凌绝顶,一览众山小。

2. White Dew starts from tonight; the moon over the hometown is brightest.

露从今夜白,月是故乡明。

3. Your bodies and names will perish, but the river will flow on forever.

尔曹身与名俱灭,不废江河万古流。

情景对话　Situational Dialogue

A: Can you tell me about Du Fu?

B: Yes. He was a great realist poet in China. He composed lots of poems concerning about the society and the people.

A: It is said that he left behind about one thousand five hundred poems. Can you tell me some of his masterpieces?

B: He composed *Parting with the Elderly*, *Parting with the Newlywed* and *Parting with the Homeless*, collectively known as *Three Part-ings*, describing the patriotic act of the ordinary people who joined the army to defend their homeland, even **humiliated**⑦.

A: I think they also expressed their concern for the fate of the Tang Dynasty and their expectation for its revival.

B: You got it. In addition, He also wrote a lot of poems to express his deep love for the common people. I remember such an impressive line, "Where can I get thousands of mansions, making all poor people share with smiles!"

A: It has moved me for a long time. You know, it was the moment when Du Fu became almost homeless, with only a broken thatched cottage left behind.

B: In my opinion, we should learn from his **patriotism**⑧ and love for the people.

A: 你能给我讲讲杜甫吗?

B: 他是中国伟大的现实主义诗人,写了许多关于社会和人民的诗。

A: 据说他留下了大约一千五百首诗。你能说出他的一些代表作吗?

B: 杜甫创作了《垂老别》《新婚别》和《无家别》,三者合称"三别",描写了普通老百姓即使蒙羞受辱也依然参军入伍保家卫国的爱国行为。

A: 我想他们也表达了自己对大唐命运的关心和对复兴的期待。

B: 你说得对。此外,杜甫还写了大量诗歌,表达了他对平民百姓的深切关爱。我记得有一句令人印象深刻的诗:"安得广厦千万间,大庇天下寒士俱欢颜!"

A: 它感动了我很长一段时间。你知道,那可是杜甫几乎无家可归的时候,身边只剩下一间破茅屋而已。

B: 在我看来,我们应该学习他的爱国精神和对人民的热爱。

生词注解 Notes

① advocate /ˈædvəkət/ *vt.* 提倡;拥护

② antithesis /ænˈtɪθəsɪs/ *n.* 对仗;对照

③ aesthetic /iːsˈθetɪk/ *adj.* 美学的;具有审美趣味的

④ upheaval /ʌpˈhiːvl/ *n.* 动乱;剧变

⑤ authentic /ɔːˈθentɪk/ *adj.* 真实的;正宗的

⑥ diversified /daɪˈvɜːsɪfaɪd/ *adj.* 多样化的;各种的

⑦ humiliated /hjuːˈmɪlieɪtɪd/ *adj.* 蒙羞的;感到自惭的

⑧ patriotism /ˈpeɪtriətɪzəm/ *n.* 爱国心;爱国精神

李商隐

Li Shangyin

导入语 Lead-in

李商隐(约813~约858),字义山,号玉溪生、樊南生,唐朝怀州河内(今河南沁阳)人,祖辈迁荥阳(今河南荥阳),晚唐著名诗人。幼年丧父,家境贫寒。进士及第后,因卷入牛李党争而遭人记恨,加上性格内向,备尝艰辛,郁郁不得志。晚唐政治腐败、官员奢靡,感伤和失望成了

当时文人心态的主流,使他形成了忧郁、敏感、清高的内心世界,并时刻流露在自己的诗歌中。他的诗歌流传下来的有六百来首。继杜甫之后,李商隐是唐代七律诗发展史上的又一里程碑,对后世产生了深远影响。

文化剪影 Cultural Outline

Li Shangyin, along with Li Bai and Li He, were known as "Three Lis". His poems were of great literary value; his twenty-two poems were collected in *The Three Hundred Tang Poems*, ranking fourth in number. His poems traced the prosperity and stability of the **prosperous**① Tang, depicted the corruption and **decadence**② of the late Tang, expressed his close attention to the social reality, and embodied his superb writing skills in parallel prose, strong patriotic enthusiasm and anti-traditional love view.

李商隐在唐朝诗坛享有盛誉,和李白、李贺并称为"三李"。李商隐的诗具有很高的文学价值,收录在《唐诗三百首》中的有二十二首,数量名列第四。他的诗歌追述了盛唐的安定繁荣,描画了晚唐的腐败颓废,表达了他对社会现实的密切关注,体现了他在骈文方面高超的创作技巧、强烈的爱国热情和反传统的爱情观。

Li Shangyin's poems were of rich and profound significance, unique in the literary style of the late Tang. On history, his poems were deep in content, subtle in words, and profound in **allusions**③. Starting with details, his poems revealed the scenes of breathtaking social dynamic state and manifested his incisive criticism of the corrupt politics. The tendency to chant history eventually became a unique delicacy in political poetry.

李商隐的诗歌意义丰富深远,在晚唐时期的文学风格上独树一帜。在咏史诗方面,其诗的特点体现为内容幽深、用词精妙、典故运用曲折深刻。他的诗从细节入手,展现了一幕幕令人惊心动魄的社会动态,表现出对腐朽政治的深刻批判。其咏史的倾向最终变成了政治诗歌中一道独特的佳肴。

Besides his poems on history, his love poems, with unique charm in poetry, have attracted the most attention from later generations. The writing of poetry in pursuit of goodness and beauty created a type of **hazy**④ aesthetics from the blurring of poetic conception; there were many **polysemy**⑤ phenomena in a poem, greatly expanding the capacity of the poem and left readers great imagination space. The **aesthete**⑥ became the father of symbolic literature for a series of untitled love poems.

除了咏史诗之外,李商隐的爱情诗独具魅力,获得后世的关注也最多。追求善美的诗歌创作开创了诗境虚化的朦胧美学,一诗多义现象众多,极大地扩充了诗歌的容量,留给读者极大的想象空间。这位唯美文学家因一系列无题爱情诗作而成为象征文学之祖。

 佳句点睛 Punchlines

1. You ask me when I can come back but I don't know, the pools in Bashan are overflowing with the autumn rain.

君问归期未有期,巴山夜雨涨秋池。

2. A spring silkworm may not stop spinning silk until death; a candle dries its tears only when it's burned down to ashes.

春蚕到死丝方尽,蜡炬成灰泪始干。

3. When this love become a beautiful recollection, what left behind with me is only **frustration**⑦.

此情可待成追忆,只是当时已惘然。

情景对话　Situational Dialogue

A: Talking about the Tang poetry, we may generally refer to such poets as Li Bai, Fairy Poet, Du Fu, Saint Poet and Bai Juyi, King of Poetry, who were all closely related to the flourishing Tang. Was there any poet much famous in the late Tang?

B: Of course. Li Shangyin was one of them.

A: You mean the founder of the Chinese symbolic poetics?

B: Yes. He is also one of the "Three Lis", the other two were Li Bai and Li He.

A: What impressed you most about his poems?

B: I'm really touched by his *To My Wife on a Rainy Night*, "When will we trim the candlewick by our west window to talk about the rainy night of Bashan?"

A: So am I. It is a love poem expressing the poet's deep longing for his wife, but he did not know his beloved wife had passed away before the letter.

B: This is indeed a typical image poem, deep in feelings, but extremely **implicit**⑧. He was really worthy of being the originator of image literature.

A: 说到唐诗,我们通常会想到"诗仙"李白、"诗圣"杜甫和"诗王"白居易等诗人,他们都与盛唐时期紧密相连。晚唐有什么著名诗人吗?

B: 当然有了,李商隐就是其中之一。

A: 你是说中国象征诗学的创始人吗?

B: 是啊。他也是"三李"之一,其他两位是李白和李贺。

A: 你对他的诗歌印象最深的是什么?

B: 他的《夜雨寄北》让我很感动:"何当共剪西窗烛,却话巴山夜雨时。"

A: 我也是。这是一首爱情诗,写的是诗人对妻子的深情思念,李商隐不知道爱妻在接到书信之前就已经离开人世了。

B: 这的确是一首典型的意象诗,情深意长,却又极为含蓄。真不愧是意象文学的鼻祖。

生词注解 Notes

① prosperous /ˈprɒspərəs/ *adj.* 繁荣的;兴旺的

② decadence /ˈdekədəns/ *n.* 颓废;堕落

③ allusion /əˈluːʒn/ *n.* 典故;暗指

④ hazy /ˈheɪzɪ/ *adj.* 朦胧的；模糊不清的

⑤ polysemy /pəˈlɪsɪmɪ/ *n.* 一词多义；多义现象

⑥ aesthete /ˈiːsθiːt/ *n.* 审美家；唯美主义者

⑦ frustration /frʌˈstreɪʃn/ *n.* 懊丧；懊恼

⑧ implicit /ɪmˈplɪsɪt/ *adj.* 含蓄的；不直接言明的

苏轼

Su Shi

 导入语　Lead-in

苏轼(1037~1101),字子瞻,号东坡居士,世称"苏东坡""苏仙"。祖籍河北栾城,眉州眉山(今四川眉山)人。生于文学世家,与苏洵、苏辙并称"三苏"。苏轼是北宋著名的文学家、政治家和书画家,自幼学习诸子百家,兼容儒释道思想,既充满强烈的入世精神,又坚持自己的政治理想,乐观旷达,进退自如,宠辱不惊,在文、诗、词方面都造诣高深,堪称宋代文学最高成就的杰出代表。他被后人誉为"唐宋八大家"之一、"宋词四大家"之一,代表作有《水调歌头·明月几时有》《赤壁赋》《念奴娇·赤壁怀古》等。林语堂说:"苏东坡是大文豪、大书法家、创新的画家。"

文化剪影 Cultural Outline

In the middle Northern Song, Su Shi was the leading figure in the literary world. He followed no set form and opened a new realm of Ci; he was the outstanding representative of the Bold and **Unrestrained**[①] School of Ci with Xin Qiji. With the passage of time, his poetic style gradually became simple and natural. He was rated as one of the "Eight Great Masters of Tang and Song", for his prose was colorful, themes were fresh and broad, and his style was free and enthusiastic. In addition, Su Shi was versed in calligraphy and painting, listed as one of the "Four Painting Families of Song" with Huang Tingjian, Mi Fu and Cai Xiang.

苏轼是北宋中期的文坛领军人物。他不拘一格,开词坛新风,和辛弃疾同为"豪放派"杰出代表。随着年龄的增长,其诗词风格逐渐变得质朴自然。他被列为"唐宋八大家"之一,其散文多姿多彩,题材清新广阔,文风自由奔放。此外,苏轼还擅长书法和绘画,与黄庭坚、米芾和蔡襄并称为"宋四家"。

Su Shi developed his own style in the creation of Ci, in which his accomplishment **surpassed**[②] his prose and poems, with a greater originality, and promoted its development in many aspects. He created an artistic technique of introducing poetry and prose into Ci; by applying a large number of prefaces and allusions, he expanded its writing horizon and realm, broke the traditional view that poetry was superior to Ci and poems were solemn but Ci was **obsequious**③, and greatly improved the literary position and artistic value of Ci.

苏轼在词创作上自成一家。他的词创作成就远超其散文和诗歌,有更大的独创性,推动了宋词诸多方面的发展。苏轼开创了以诗入词、以文入词的艺术手法,大量运用序言和典故,扩大了词的创作视野,开阔了词的境界,破除了诗尊词卑、诗庄词媚的传统见解,大大提高了词的文学地位和艺术价值。

Su Shi's political essays, with lofty ideas, had a great **momentum**④, and in the meanwhile, he was good at using plain and vivid metaphors to **illustrate**⑤ the profound principles while the language was natural and smooth, popular and easy to understand. Su Shi valued the ideological level of the literary works; in addition to the perfect combination of narration and **lyricism**⑥, there were often some naturally enlightening comments to embody his philosophic ideas.

苏轼的政论文文笔纵横,立意高远,具有磅礴的气势,同时又善于运用浅显生动的比喻来阐释深刻的道理,语言自然流畅,内容通俗易懂。苏轼注重文学作品的思想性,除了记叙和抒情的完美融合,常常会有一些自然而然醍醐灌顶的评论,以体现其哲学思想。

佳句点睛 Punchlines

1. Life is a reverse journey, and I am also on my way.

人生如逆旅,我亦是行人。

2. Wish we could live a long life and share the beauty despite a thousand miles away.

但愿人长久,千里共婵娟。

3. The true face of Lushan is lost to my sight, for it is right in this mountain I reside.

不识庐山真面目,只缘身在此山中。

 情景对话　Situational Dialogue

A: I remember Wang Guowei stated in his *Comments on Ci in the Human World* that "Comparing the Song Ci poetry with the Tang poems, Dongpo was like Taibai ..."

B: It has fully illustrated Su Shi's literary influence. It was Su Shi who put forth the idea that "poetry and Ci are one family".

A: I admire his literary achievements, but I think he was an architect.

B: An architect? What do you mean?

A: Do you know there is a long dike running through West Lake in Hangzhou, Zhejiang?

B: Yes. It is very convenient for travelers to enjoy the beautiful scenery of West Lake.

A: It was initiated by Su Shi. Because of his great contributions, the long dike was named after him, known as Su Dike. But this was just one of his projects.

B: You mean there are others.

A: Yes. Besides, he also built two other dikes in Fuyang, Anhui and Huiyang, Guangdong. **Coincidentally**[⑦], the two completed projects are called "West Lake".

B: It seems that Su Dongpo had a preference for the name of West Lake.

A: Yes. But what attracts me more is that Su Dongpo built the first dike when he was head of Hangzhou and the other two during his **banishment**[⑧].

B: Thus, Su Dongpo was an architect for the people. He didn't forget to benefit the common people, whether in rain or shine.

A: 我记得王国维在《人间词话》里说:"以宋词比唐诗,则东坡似太白……"

B: 这充分证明了苏轼的文学影响力,是苏轼提出了"诗词一家"的思想。

A: 我钦佩他的文学成就,但我认为他是一位建筑师。

B: 建筑师?此话怎讲?

A: 你知道有一条长堤贯穿浙江杭州的西湖吗?

B: 知道,它便于游客欣赏西湖美景。

A: 它是由苏东坡发起建造的。因其巨大贡献,该长堤就以他的名字命名,世人称之为"苏堤"。而这不过是其设计的一个工程。

B: 你是说还有其他的?

A: 是啊。除此之外,苏东坡还建造了另外两个"苏堤",分别在安徽阜阳和广东惠阳。巧合的是,两处工程竣工之所都叫"西湖"。

B: 看来,苏东坡对"西湖"这个名字是情有独钟啊。

A: 是的。更吸引我的是,苏东坡建造第一个长堤时是杭州通判,而建造其他两处则是在贬谪期间。

B: 如此说来,苏东坡还是一位"人民建筑师",宠辱不忘造福百姓。

生词注解　Notes

① unrestrained /ˌʌnrɪˈstreɪnd/　*adj.* 无拘无束的

② surpass /səˈpɑːs/　*vt.* 超过;胜过

③ obsequious /əbˈsiːkwɪəs/　*adj.* 谄媚的;奉承的

④ momentum /məˈmentəm/　*n.* 冲力;势头

⑤ illustrate /ˈɪləstreɪt/　*vt.* 阐明;举例说明

⑥ lyricism /ˈlɪrɪsɪzəm/　*n.* 抒情性;抒情诗体

⑦ coincidentally /kəʊˌɪnsɪˈdentəlɪ/　*adv.* 巧合地;碰巧地

⑧ banishment /ˈbænɪʃmənt/　*n.* 流放;充军

吴承恩

Wu Cheng'en

导入语 Lead-in

吴承恩(约1500～1583),字汝中,号射阳山人。淮安府山阳县(今江苏淮安)人,明朝杰出小说家。自幼敏慧,酷爱神话故事,下笔成文,但科举不顺,年届五旬方补岁贡生,六十任县丞,官场失意,不久愤而辞任,著书立说,代表作有《西游记》《禹鼎记》《射阳集》。《西游记》取材于《大唐西域记》《大唐三藏取经诗话》《唐三藏》《蟠桃会》《大唐大慈恩寺三藏法师传》《唐三藏西天取经》《二郎神锁齐大圣》等,是中国文学史上一部杰出的神魔小说,也是魔幻现实主义的开山之作。

 文化剪影 Cultural Outline

When he was young, Wu Cheng'en was talented and well-known far and near. He had a photographic memory for reading, he could dash off a poem or prose in a flash, he had a wide range of hobbies, and he was proficient in painting and calligraphy. Though mostly lost, Wu Cheng'en wrote many works, collected and edited later into four volumes of *Mr. Sheyang's Manuscripts*, where there are respectively nearly one hundred pieces in poetry and Ci, giving direct expression to inner feelings and rich in "the literary style of Li Bai and Xin Qiji". In terms of novel writing, he could separate himself from the **revivalism**①, emphasize the removal of **pompous**② words, create refreshing articles, and shaped the romantic heroic spirit of *Journey to the West*.

吴承恩少有才华,闻名遐迩,读书过目不忘,诗文一挥而就,爱好广泛,精通绘画和书法。吴承恩著作甚丰,尽管大多散失,仍被后人搜集编成《射阳先生存稿》四卷存世。书中诗词各有近百篇,直抒胸臆,富于"李辛遗风"。小说创作方面,他能让自己与复古主义剥离,强调去除华而不实之辞,创作令人耳目一新之文,塑造了《西游记》的浪漫英雄主义气概。

Wu Cheng'en's most well-known literary legacy was certainly *Journey to the West*. It is said that in order to complete the novel, Wu Cheng'en traveled faraway through famous mountains and great rivers, from which he collected a lot of materials about immortals and evil spirits. Taking as the clue that the Tang Monk journeyed to the west for the Buddhist scriptures, the book described a legend of how to **subdue**③ and eliminate the demons all the way, how to go through the eighty-one **adversities**④ and how to reap the real scriptures eventually. As soon as the novel came out, it became a household word.

吴承恩最著名的文化遗产当然非《西游记》莫属。为完成《西游记》，吴承恩远游名山大川，积累了大量神仙鬼怪故事素材。该书以唐僧西天取经为线索，描述了一路降妖除魔，历经九九八十一难，终于取得真经的传奇故事。小说一经问世，便家喻户晓。

Journey to the West is the first traditional Chinese fantasy novel, marking the peak of ancient Chinese romantic novels both in ideology and art. Through romanticism, the novel created a **fantastic**⑤ and magnificent mythological world full of humors and amusements; by interweaving the ideas of Confucianism, Taoism and Buddhism and blending the features of deity, humanity and naturality, it **pioneered**⑥ the creation of the world's novels of magic realism.

《西游记》是中国第一部章回体神魔长篇小说，无论在思想上还是在艺术上，都标志着中国古代浪漫主义长篇小说的巅峰。小说通过浪漫主义手法创造了一个奇幻瑰丽、妙趣横生的神话世界，通过儒、道、佛思想的交错，神性、人性和自然性的融合，开创了世界魔幻现实主义小说的先河。

 ## 佳句点睛　Punchlines

1. Nothing is impossible to a willing heart.

世上无难事，只怕有心人。

2. Return the borrowed things on time and you'll be welcome next time.

好借好还，再借不难。

3. To achieve a great cause, we must fight against all kinds of ghosts and monsters.

要成就伟业，就必须与各路妖魔鬼怪进行斗争。

 ## 情景对话　Situational Dialogue

A: Do you know who is Wu Cheng'en?

B: He was the author of *Journey to the West*, which was the first traditional Chinese novel about immortals and ghosts, marking the pinnacle of the romantic ancient Chinese novels.

A: It has been made into TV series, as well as films and cartoons.

B: Yes. True classics can always be **fascinating**[①]. As far as I know, the earliest movie about it was perhaps *The Cave of the Silken Web* released to the public in Norway in 1929. And the most influential may be *The Monkey King*.

A: I love the Monkey King.

B: Since the cartoon movie ***Havoc*** ⑧ ***in Heaven***, it has captured the hearts of people of all ages.

A: But I think it a little tragic.

B: What do you mean?

A: You know that though he **vanquished**⑨ evil spirits more than once, the Monkey King was finally suppressed at the foot of the Five-Element Mountain.

B: Oh, I see. That's why we admire him as a hero. "In the face of a strong opponent, knowing that he is defeated, he should resolutely show his sword. Even if he falls down, he should also become a mountain"! How awe-inspiring!

A: 你知道吴承恩是谁吗?

B: 他是《西游记》的作者。《西游记》是中国第一部章回体神魔小说,也是中国古代浪漫主义小说的巅峰之作。

A: 它已被拍成了电视剧,还有电影和动画片呢。

B: 是啊,真正的经典总是能引人入胜。据我所知,关于《西游记》最早的电影或许是《盘丝洞》,它于1929年在挪威公映。而最有影响的电影大概是《美猴王》。

A: 我非常喜爱那个美猴王。

B: 卡通电影《大闹天宫》自上映以来,就俘获了各个年龄段观众的心。

A: 可我认为它有点儿悲剧。

B: 何出此言？

A: 你知道，尽管美猴王不止一次降服妖魔鬼怪，但他最终还是被镇压在了五行山下。

B: 噢，我明白了。这也正是我们视他为英雄的原因。"面对强大的对手，明知不敌，也要毅然亮剑，即使倒下，也要成为一座山"！这是何等的凛然！

生词注解 Notes

① revivalism /rɪˈvaɪvəlɪzəm/ n. 复兴；宗教复兴运动

② pompous /ˈpɒmpəs/ adj. 言辞浮夸的；虚华的

③ subdue /səbˈdjuː/ vt. 制伏；降服

④ adversity /ədˈvɜːsətɪ/ n. 困境；逆境

⑤ fantastic /fænˈtæstɪk/ adj. 富于想象的；荒诞不经的

⑥ pioneer /ˌpaɪəˈnɪə(r)/ vt. 开辟；倡导

⑦ fascinating /ˈfæsɪneɪtɪŋ/ adj. 引人入胜的；极有吸引力的

⑧ havoc /ˈhævək/ n. 浩劫；祸患

⑨ vanquish /ˈvæŋkwɪʃ/ vt. 完胜；彻底击败

曹雪芹

Cao Xueqin

导入语 Lead-in

曹雪芹(约1715~约1763)，本名曹霑，字梦阮，号雪芹、芹溪、芹圃。祖籍辽宁铁岭，生于江宁(今江苏南京)，清代著名小说家。生于繁华，终于困顿。幼时因出身高官贵胄而锦衣玉食，青少年因被抄家而随家北迁，回到北京后靠卖字画和友人接济为生。晚年居住在北京西郊，"满径蓬蒿"，生活更无着落，"举家食粥酒常赊"，在友人郭诚的劝说下，专心著书，十年如一日，披阅旧作《风月宝鉴》，先后"增删五次"，最终写成了皇皇巨著《红楼梦》。该书堪称中国古代长篇小说的巅峰之作，在世界文学史上占有举足轻重的地位。中国红楼梦学会会长、

《红楼梦学刊》主编张庆善说:"曹雪芹是中国最伟大的作家,他值得中国人民缅怀、纪念。因为他是《红楼梦》的作者,是中华民族文化的象征。……它永远矗立在世界文学的珠穆朗玛峰上,是中华民族的骄傲"。

文化剪影　Cultural Outline

Though ill-fated, Cao Xueqin was open-minded in character, had a wide range of interests and not only made uncommon studies in poetry, painting, customs, health-preserving, gardening and economy, but also created the **monumental**① work *A Dream of Red Mansions*, which through the fire of literature offers warmth, shows sincerity to people and makes them brave and strong to part with the old society in experiencing the human **inconstancy**② and understanding the decay of the feudal system. The profound thought, exquisite art and everlasting charm embodied in *A Dream of Red Mansions* can make it comparable with any literary classic in the world.

曹雪芹虽命运多舛,但性格豁达,爱好广泛,不仅在诗词、绘画、风俗、养生、园林、经济等方面都颇有研究,而且写出了恢弘巨著《红楼梦》,用文学之火给人以温暖,示人以真情,让人在体验世态炎凉之中,在认识封建腐朽没落之时,产生诀别旧社会、旧制度的勇气和力量。《红楼梦》所体现的深邃思想、精湛艺术和永恒魅力,可与世界上任何一部文学经典相比肩。

A Dream of Red Mansions, originally known as *The Story of the Stone*, was a traditional Chinese novel, which was large in scale, numerous in character, and well-structured, with two versions of one hundred and twenty chapters, and eighty chapters. Since its **publication**③, it has been regarded as a treasure, popular in China, forming a rare phenomenon of "Redology" in the history of Chinese literature.

《红楼梦》又名《石头记》,是一部中国古典小说。小说规模宏大、人物众多、结构严谨,有一百二十回和八十回两种版本。该书一经问世,便被视为珍品,风靡华夏,形成了中国文学史上罕见的"红学"现象。

A Dream of Red Mansions was a novel of human relations, taking the love and marriage tragedy of Jia Baoyu, Lin Daiyu and Xue Baochai as the clue; and in the background of the rise and fall of Jia, Wang, Shi and Xue families, it described the human beauty and ugliness, and the social **fickleness**④, revealed the decline of the dynasty, truthfully illustrated various inevitable tragedies of the people from the aristocratic to the nameless under the feudal ethnics, and **comprehensively**⑤ depicted the vast historical picture of the feudal society from the palace to the countryside.

《红楼梦》是一部人情小说,以贾宝玉、林黛玉和薛宝钗的恋情婚姻悲剧为线索,在贾、王、史、薛四大家族兴衰的背景下,描写了人情美丑、世态炎凉,揭示了王朝衰败,如实展示了封建伦理中上至贵族、下至无名小卒的各种必然悲剧,全面描述了封建社会中上至宫廷、下

至乡村的广阔历史画卷。

佳句点睛 Punchlines

1. A grasp of **mundane**① affairs is genuine knowledge, while understanding of worldly wisdom is true learning.

世事洞明皆学问，人情练达即文章。

2. When false is taken for true, true becomes false; if non-being turns into being, being becomes non-being.

假作真时真亦假，无为有处有还无。

3. When you have money, you would never look ahead; when you have none, you would fly into a temper.

有了钱就顾头不顾尾，没了钱就瞎生气。

情景对话 Situational Dialogue

A: You've been learning about Chinese literature for a long time. What do you know about Cao Xueqin?

B: He is one of the great writers most worthy of remembering in China.

A: Why do you think so?

B: I have three reasons for that.

A: Share them with me.

B: First, he is a gifted literary figure who was born in **prosperity**⑦ and ended in poverty, but he did not stop his literary creation.

A: And the second?

B: He completed *A Dream of Red Mansions* with great **perseverance**⑧.

A: What about the third reason then?

B: Also for his *A Dream of Red Mansion*. The work is so all-inclusive that is almost an encyclopedia.

A: Cao was really a great novelist in the Chinese literature.

B: I agree with you.

A: 你学习中国文学好长时间了，你对曹雪芹有多少了解呢？

B: 他是中国值得纪念的伟大作家之一。

A: 为什么这么说呢？

B: 我有三条理由。

A: 请跟我分享一下吧。

B: 首先，他是一位才华出众的文学家，生于富贵，终于贫困，却没有放弃他的文学创作。

A: 第二个理由呢？

B: 其次，他以坚忍不拔的毅力完成了《红楼梦》。

A: 第三个理由呢？

B: 还是因为他的《红楼梦》。这部作品包罗万象，简直就是一部百科全书。

A: 这么说来，曹雪芹真是一位伟大的小说家。
B: 我赞成你的看法。

生词注解　Notes

① monumental /ˌmɒnjuˈmentl/　*adj.* 不朽的；宏伟的

② inconstancy /ɪnˈkɒnstənsɪ/　*n.* 反复无常；不确定

③ publication /ˌpʌblɪˈkeɪʃn/　*n.*（书刊等的）出版；发表

④ fickleness /ˈfɪklnəs/　*n.* 变化无常；易变

⑤ comprehensively /ˌkɒmprɪˈhensɪvlɪ/　*adv.* 完全地；彻底地

⑥ mundane /mʌnˈdeɪn/　*adj.* 单调的；平凡的

⑦ prosperity /prɒˈsperətɪ/　*n.* 繁荣；兴旺

⑨ perseverance /ˌpɜːsɪˈvɪərəns/　*n.* 毅力；不屈不挠

鲁迅

Lu Xun

 导入语　Lead-in

鲁迅(1881~1936),原名周树人,浙江绍兴人。中国现代著名文学家、思想家和革命家,中国现代文学的奠基人,新文化运动的先驱,中国翻译文学的伟大开拓者。少年家道中落,历经世态炎凉。从日本归国后,为民族救亡图存而弃医从文,加盟《新青年》,支持革命加入"左联",一生致力于改变国民精神,被誉为"二十世纪东亚文化地图上占最大领土的作家",代表作有《阿Q正传》《祝福》《孔乙己》《故乡》《药》《野草》《朝花夕拾》《呐喊》《华盖集》《热风》《中国小说史略》等。毛泽东评价鲁迅是"中国文化革命的主将,鲁迅的骨头是最硬的,鲁迅的方向就

是中华民族新文化的方向"。大江健三郎评价鲁迅是"二十世纪亚洲最伟大的作家"。

 文化剪影　Cultural Outline

Lu Xun was a world cultural giant in the twentieth century, honored as the founder of modern Chinese literature, the pioneer in translated literature, the forerunner of the modern ideological emancipation and the great mentor in the new style woodcut movement, and his literary status and ideological influence are renowned at home and abroad, especially in Japan and the Korean Peninsula. His masterworks include *Call to Arms*, *Wandering*, *Old Tales Retold*, *A Madman's Diary*, *Wild Grass*, *Dawn Blossoms* **Plucked**① *at Dusk*, *Unlucky Star*, *A Brief History of Chinese Fiction*, and so on.

鲁迅是二十世纪世界文化巨擘,被誉为中国现代文学的奠基人、翻译文学的开拓者、现代思想解放的先驱和新型版画运动的伟大导师,其地位和思想影响蜚声海内外,尤其是在日本和朝鲜半岛。他的代表作有《呐喊》《彷徨》《故事新编》《狂人日记》《野草》《朝花夕拾》《华盖集》《中国小说史略》等。

Lu Xun's essays were rich in content, known as encyclopedia, with strong characteristics of the times, critical thoughts and fighting spirit. *A Madman's Diary* pioneered modern **vernacular**② Chinese and embodied the fruits of the New Culture Movement. Mao Zedong commented,

"Lu Xun's direction is that of the new culture of the Chinese nation."

鲁迅的杂文内容丰富,被誉为百科全书,有强烈的时代特征,富于批判思想和战斗精神。他的《狂人日记》开中国现代白话文的先声,体现出新文化运动的成果。毛泽东评价说:"鲁迅的方向,就是中华民族新文化的方向。"

Lu Xun's literary creation had its own distinctive characteristics. He preferred peasants and **intellectuals**③ as the major subjects in the fiction, focusing on the analyses of psychological **trauma**④ and social crisis. He also drew on a variety of artistic experience, integrated into the national style and created poetic fiction, prose-style fiction and dramatic fiction. His essays had a strong sense of the times; starting with *Hot Wind*, his essays criticized feudal **ethics**⑤ and old traditions, which were almost a history of ideological and cultural struggle.

鲁迅的文学作品特色鲜明。他的小说首选农民和知识分子为主要题材,注重剖析精神创伤和社会危机。他还借鉴各种艺术经验,融入民族风貌,创立"诗化小说""散文体小说"和"戏剧化小说"。他的杂文时代感强,从杂文集《热风》开始,批判封建礼教和旧传统,简直就是一部思想文化斗争史。

佳句点睛 Punchlines

1. When thought spread wide to fill the whole space, amid the silence comes the crash of thunder.

心事浩茫连广宇，于无声处听惊雷。

2. If you don't explode in silence, you'll perish in silence.

不在沉默中爆发，就在沉默中灭亡。

3. In fact, there is no way in the world. With more people walking, it will become a way.

其实世上本没有路，走的人多了，也便成了路。

情景对话　Situational Dialogue

A: I'm planning to take a cultural tour in Shanghai this summer.

B: You can visit Lu Xun Museum.

A: Lu Xun? I know he was a great literary figure. But his hometown is Shaoxing, Zhejiang. How can there be Lu Xun Museum in Shanghai?

B: Lu Xun was more than a common literary **celebrity**[⑥]. He was more of a democratic forerunner and revolutionary soldier. Most of his late years was spent there writing for national independence.

A: So the museum was built. Shanghai deserves the Capital of Revolution.

B: Lu Xun's essays are called the "the history of ideological and cultural struggle". I think visiting there will impress you not only upon his traces of life but also the cultural course of modern China.

A: In this case, tell me more about Lu Xun.

B: He was knowns the founder of modern Chinese literature, the forerunner of the modern ideological liberation and the great mentor in the New Culture Movement.

A: What's your deepest impression of Lu Xun? I've heard a lot about *A Madman's Diary*.

B: It was the first vernacular Chinese short story. But I admire most his **determination**⑦ to give up medicine and engage into literature.

A: So do I.

B: Only by reforming people's minds can there be a bright national future.

A: Lu Xun deserved a cultural giant of the twentieth century. I'm sure I'll have an impressive cultural tour. Thank you.

B: My pleasure. Have a nice trip!

A：我计划今年夏天去上海来趟文化之旅。

B：你不妨参观一下鲁迅博物馆。

A：鲁迅？我知道他是一位伟大的文学人物。可是他的家乡在浙江绍兴，怎么上海会有鲁迅博物馆呢？

B：鲁迅可不仅仅是一般的文化名人，他更是一位民主先驱和革命斗士。他晚年大部分时光都是在上海度过的，为民族独立而写作。

A：因此上海建立了鲁迅博物馆，上海称得上是革命之都。

B：鲁迅的杂文被称为"思想文化的斗争史"。我想，拜访那里将会让你对他的人生痕迹和现代中国的文化进程都留下深刻印象。

A: 既然这样，请你给我多讲讲鲁迅吧。

B: 他被誉为现代中国文学的奠基人、现代思想解放的先驱和新文化运动的伟大导师。

A: 你对鲁迅最深的印象是什么？我知道《狂人日记》。

B: 它是中国第一部白话文短篇小说。但是，我最钦佩他弃医从文的决心。

A: 我也是。

B: 只有改造人民的思想，民族才有光明的未来。

A: 鲁迅不愧为二十世纪的文化巨人。我一定会有个印象深刻的文化之旅。谢谢你。

B: 不客气。祝你旅途愉快！

生词注解 Notes

① pluck /plʌk/ *vt.* 摘；拔掉

② vernacular /vəˈnækjələ(r)/ *adj.* 本国的；方言的

③ intellectual /ˌɪntəˈlektʃuəl/ *n.* 知识分子

④ trauma /ˈtrɔːmə/ *n.* (心理导致的精神失常)创伤；外伤

⑤ ethics /ˈeθɪks/ *n.* 礼教；道德原则

⑥ celebrity /səˈlebrətɪ/ *n.* 名人；名望

⑦ determination /dɪˌtɜːmɪˈneɪʃn/ *n.* 决心；果断

巴金

Ba Jin

导入语 Lead-in

巴金（1904~2005），本名李尧棠，字芾甘，四川成都人，祖籍浙江嘉兴。中国现代杰出的文学家、出版家、翻译家和社会活动家。巴金生于封建家庭，从小嗜书如命，受五四运动影响，求学南京、上海，青年时期留学法国，喜西方哲学、文学，同时关心祖国命运，开始文学创作。抗战时，与茅盾主编《呐喊》，辗转各地进行抗日文化宣传。新中国成立后先后任中国作协主席、政协副主席，笔耕不辍，获"人民作家"称号，被誉为"二十世纪中国文学的良心"，代表作有《家》《寒夜》《随想录》等。王蒙说："他是我们的一面旗帜，也是榜样。"

 文化剪影　Cultural Outline

Ba Jin was a **prolific**① writer, who took active part in various social activities throughout his life and whose works often went with the times, merely valuing truth and kindness. Looking through his one hundred years of life, he published with twenty-two novelettes and novels, fifteen short story collections, thirty-seven prose collections, twenty literary translations, fourteen biographies, ten **theoretical**② works, and sixteen theoretical translations. In addition, he also edited seventeen literary magazines successively.

巴金是一位多产作家,一生积极参与各类社会活动,其作品与时俱进,唯真唯善。纵观其百年人生,巴金发表和出版的中长篇小说有22部、短篇小说集15部、散文集37部、文学译著20部、传记作品14部、理论作品10部、理论译著16部。此外,他还先后主编过17种文学杂志。

Ba Jin reaped countless classical works and applauses. His masterpieces included the novels, such as *Family*, *Spring*, *Autumn* and *Cold Nights*, short story collections, such as *Revenge*, *Light*, *The Longevity Pagoda*③ and *Stories of the Heroes*, the last of which was Ba Jin's great contribution to the literary development of New China. Francois Mitterand, president of the Republic of France, regarded Ba Jin as "one of the greatest witnesses of the (twenty) century".

巴金一生名作无数,赞誉无数。代表作有长篇小说《家》《春》《秋》《寒夜》,短篇小说集《复仇集》《光明集》《长生塔》和《英雄的故事》,其中《英雄的故事》是巴金对新中国文学发展的重要贡献。法国总统密特朗认为巴金是"本世纪(20世纪)伟大的见证人之一"。

Ba Jin's fictions had various themes and colorful contents, displaying the historical development process of society. His novelettes and novels **delineated**④ the most beautiful scenery in the 1930s. His novels were versed in expressing the conflicts and ups and downs of families, reflecting time changes, such as *The Torrent*⑤ *Trilogy*; his short stories contained the vivid descriptions of foreigners and the suffering struggles of people from all walks of life, the historical **perception**⑥ of the French revolution and the willingness of the volunteer soldiers as well as the basic necessities of life for the common people and the vision of a fairyland.

巴金的小说题材多样,内容多彩,表现了社会历史的发展进程。他的小说勾画出了20世纪30年代最明媚的风景。他的中长篇小说善写家庭矛盾和浮沉,折射时代的变迁,如"激流三部曲";他的短篇小说既有对外国人的生动描述,又有各阶层人民苦难的抗争历程,既有对法国大革命的历史感知,又描写了志愿军战士的义无反顾,既有小人物的衣食住行,又有童话世界里的美好愿景。

佳句点睛 Punchlines

1. In order to pursue light and heat, people would rather give up their life.

为着追求光和热,人宁愿舍弃自己的生命。

2. I love my country and my people, and without the former or the latter, I cannot survive or write.

我爱我的祖国,爱我的人民,离开了它,离开了他们,我就无法生存,更无法写作。

3. I should by no means feel **pessimistic**[①]. I will endeavor to live longer. I will work for our socialist homeland until my last breath.

我绝不悲观。我要争取多活。我要为我们的社会主义祖国工作到生命的最后一息。

情景对话 Situational Dialogue

A: Shall we have a talk about Ba Jin?

B: Very good. I'm a real Ba Jin fan.

A: Why did he use "Ba Jin"?

B: It is the pen name when he published his first novel *Destruction*.

A: *Destruction*? Why did he use that name?

B: The novel was published in 1929, which was a bloody and dark time. Ba Jin was a man to speak truth and seek light. It's of no wonder to reflect the decade with a striking title.

A: What do you think about his *Torrent Trilogy*?

B: The trilogy can be his outstanding masterpieces, of which *Family* was the most influential. If *Destruction* was his first cornerstone, *Family* would be his first **monument**⑧ on his road to literature.

A: Ba Jin might be a great writer best at telling the changes of society by writing the story of family. He also wrote a book, titled *Random*⑨ *Thoughts*. Do you know?

B: Yes, I do. They were more than one hundred and fifty essays written by Ba Jin from 1978 to 1986. It was a penetrating collection of prose that can stand for the highest achievement of Chinese contemporary literature.

A: There was one impressive statement, "No way, and today we must greatly fight against feudalism."

B: Ba Jin devoted his whole life to the cause of anti-feudalism.

A: 咱们可以聊聊巴金吗？

B: 好啊。我可是个实实在在的巴金迷呢。

A: 为什么要用"巴金"这个笔名呢？

B: 这是他发表第一部小说《灭亡》时用的笔名。

A:《灭亡》？为什么用那样一个名字？

B: 小说发表于1929年，那是个血腥黑暗的年代。巴金是位讲真话、求光明之人。用这个显眼的标题反映那十年并不奇怪。

A: 你认为他的"激流三部曲"怎么样?

B: 三部曲都是他杰出的代表作,其中《家》最有影响。如果说《灭亡》是其文学道路的第一块奠基石,《家》就是第一座丰碑。

A: 巴金最擅长通过写家庭故事来反映社会变迁。巴金还有一本书叫《随想录》,你知道吗?

B: 是的,我知道。这是巴金于1978年至1986年写的150余篇随笔,是一部力透纸背、能够代表中国当代文学最高成就的散文集。

A: 里边有一句话让人印象深刻:"没有办法,今天我们还必须大反封建。"

B: 巴金把整个人生都奉献给了反封建事业。

生词注解 Notes

① theoretical /ˌθɪəˈretɪkl/ *adj.* 理论的;理论上的

② prolific /prəˈlɪfɪk/ *adj.* 多产的;丰富的

③ pagoda /pəˈɡəʊdə/ *n.* (东亚或南亚的)佛塔

④ delineate /dɪˈlɪnieɪt/ *vt.* 描绘;详细解释

⑤ torrent /ˈtɒrənt/ *n.* 激流;湍流

⑥ perception /pəˈsepʃn/ *n.* 感悟;感知

⑦ pessimistic /ˌpesɪˈmɪstɪk/ *adj.* 悲观的;悲观主义的

⑧ monument /ˈmɒnjumənt/ *n.* 纪念碑;不朽的作品

⑨ random /ˈrændəm/ *adj.* 随机的;随意的

金庸

Louis Cha

导入语 Lead-in

金庸(1924~2018),本名查良镛,浙江海宁人,祖籍江西婺源。著名武侠小说家、政论家和社会活动家,香港四大才子之一。生于书香门第,幼年痴迷武侠,中学编写第一本书《给投考初中者》,大学先后就读于重庆和上海,毕业后任《大公报》翻译,后被调往香港。1955年出版《书剑恩仇录》时署名"金庸",此后作品不断,成为新派武侠小说杰出代表。后创办《明报》,投身社会事务。代表作有《书剑恩仇录》《射雕英雄传》《雪山飞狐》《神雕侠侣》《倚天屠龙记》《天龙八部》《笑傲江湖》《鹿鼎记》等。1998年,金庸获文学创作终身成就奖。2001年,国际天文

杰出人物

学会将一颗由北京天文台发现的编号10930的小行星命名为"金庸"。

文化剪影 Cultural Outline

Born in a noble family and influenced by his father, Louis Cha was fond of *The Legends of Water Marsh* and *Seven Chivalrous Heroes and Five Righteous Men* as a boy. Since the publication of the first wuxia novel *The Book and the Sword* in 1955, he completed *The Deer and the **Cauldron***①, *The Legend of the **Condor**② Heroes*, *The Demi-Gods and Semi-Devils*, *Fox Volant of the Snowy Mountain*, *The Return of the Condor Heroes*, and so on, which **triggered**③ waves of wulin whirlwinds in the literary and artistic realm. He successively initiated five kinds of newspapers, including *Ming Pao*, and two publishing houses.

金庸出身名门望族,受父亲影响,自幼喜读《水浒传》和《七侠五义》。自从1955年其第一部武侠小说《书剑恩仇录》问世后,金庸完成了《鹿鼎记》《射雕英雄传》《天龙八部》《雪山飞狐》《神雕侠侣》等作品,在文艺界引发了一波又一波的武林旋风。他先后创办《明报》等五种报刊以及两个出版社。

Louis Cha was not only a prominent figure in the newspaper industry, but also a leading figure in the new wuxia novels, recognized as a master of popular literature. By virtue of his profound historical knowledge, intense national spirit and rich cultural **ambience**④, he created wuxia classics one after another, launched a silent literary revolution and established a new school of martial arts novels, which make wuxia novels step into the palace of Chinese literature with dignity.

金庸不仅是报业杰出人士,也是新派武侠小说的领军人物,被公认为通俗文学大师。凭借深厚的历史知识、强烈的民族精神和丰富的文化气息,金庸创作了一部又一部脍炙人口的武侠经典,悄无声息地发动了一场文学革命,开新派武侠小说先河,使武侠小说顺利跻身中国文学的殿堂。

As the representatives of popular literature, Louis Cha's novels were distinctive in both thought and culture. First of all, there was an expansive historical space integrated in the novels, unfolding a chain of historical settings on end, where historic figures and literary characters competed on the same stage, such as Zhu Yuanzhang and Zhang Wuji, Kangxi and Wei Xiaobao. Secondly, there were a variety of **conflicts**[5] designed to construct various tragedies and reveal an ideological pursuit of the chivalrous heroes, to serve the country and the people by using the **entanglements**[6] in personal emotions, constant disputes among wushu sects, and the national turmoil, such as Guo Jing, Chen Jialuo and Qiao Feng. Thirdly, he created various female roles with clear love and hate, seeking either personal freedom or traditional virtue, reflecting the cultural pursuit of the unity of opposites.

作为通俗文学的代表,金庸的小说无论是在思想上还是在文化上都具有鲜明的特色。首先是融入广阔的历史空间,不断展现一系列历史场景,让历史人物和文学角色同台竞技,比如朱元璋和张无忌、康熙和韦小宝。其次是设立多种冲突,利用个人情感纠结、武林门派纷争和国家民族动荡构建各种悲剧,并揭示为国为民的侠客的思想追求,比如郭靖、陈家洛和乔峰。第三是创造了多种多样爱憎分明的女性角色,她们或求个人自由,或求传统美德,体现出对立统一的文化追求。

佳句点睛 Punchlines

1. In his way, give back to him.

以彼之道,还施彼身。

2. A love that shocks the world would always cost a lot.

惊世骇俗的爱情总是要付出许多代价。

3. The greatness of **chivalrous**① swordsmen lies in that they serve the country and the people.

侠之大者,为国为民。

情景对话 Situational Dialogue

A: Do you know Louis Cha?

B: He was a famous novelist. What about you?

A: I read his *The Legend of the Condor Heroes*, which attracted

me so much that I often stayed up late reading.

B: So did I.

A: What puzzled me was the so-called Jianghu.

B: I also got it later from another novel *The Smiling Proud Wanderer*, that where there're people, there would be feelings of gratitude and **resentment**®, where there're old scores, there would be Jianghu.

A: Well said. One cannot live without society. Since it is a Jianghu, there should be various types of people. Some are absorbed into wushu classics, some are addicted to wine and beauty, some are desperate for power, and some will die for justice.

B: What do you like most about Louis Cha's novels?

A: As far as characterization is concerned, I like Guo Jing most, the hero stuck to one idea that "the greatness of chivalrous swordsmen lies in that they serve the country and the people".

B: It should be one of the most shining themes in Louis Cha.

A: Right. Chen Jialuo in *The Book and the Sword*, Yang Guo in *The Return of the Condor Heroes*, and Qiao Feng in *The Demi-Gods and Semi-Devils* are all such types. In that case, Louis Cha could be a **patriotic**⑨ novelist.

B: I agree with you.

A: 你了解金庸吗？

B: 他是一位著名的小说家。你了解他吗？

A: 我读过他的《射雕英雄传》，我经常熬夜阅读、沉迷其中。

B: 我也一样。

A: 让我迷惑不解的就是那个所谓的江湖。

B: 我后来从另一本小说《笑傲江湖》里明白了,只要有人的地方就有恩怨,有恩怨就会有江湖。

A: 说得好。个人的生活离不开社会。既然是江湖,那就会有各种人等。有人沉浸于武学宝典,有人沉迷于酒色,有人为权势铤而走险,有人则舍生取义。

B: 你最喜欢金庸小说的什么方面呢?

A: 就人物刻画而言,我最喜欢郭靖,这位英雄坚守一种思想,就是"侠之大者,为国为民。"

B: 这应该是金庸小说中闪亮的主题之一。

A: 对,《书剑恩仇录》里的陈家洛、《神雕侠侣》中的杨过和《天龙八部》里的乔峰都是这种类型。这么说来,金庸可算是爱国小说家了。

B: 我同意你的看法。

生词注解 Notes

① cauldron /ˈkɔːldrən/ *n.* 大锅;煮皂锅

② condor /ˈkɒndɔː(r)/ *n.* 神鹰;大秃鹰

③ trigger /ˈtrɪɡə(r)/ *vt.* 触发;引起

④ ambience /ˈæmbɪəns/ *n.* 氛围;格调

⑤ conflict /ˈkɒnflɪkt/ *n.* 冲突;争论

⑥ entanglement /ɪnˈtæŋglmənt/　*n.* 瓜葛;纠缠
⑦ chivalrous /ˈʃɪvəlrəs/　*adj.* 侠义的;骑士的
⑧ resentment /rɪˈzentmənt/　*n.* 愤恨;怨恨
⑨ patriotic /ˌpeɪtriˈɒtɪk/　*adj.* 爱国的

第六部分 艺术大师

Part Ⅵ Great Masters of Art

王羲之

Wang Xizhi

导入语 Lead-in

王羲之（303～361），字逸少，又称"王右军"，琅琊临沂（今山东临沂）人，后迁居会稽山阴（今浙江绍兴）。东晋著名书法家。王羲之出身魏晋名门，自幼酷爱书法绘画，早年师承卫夫人，学钟繇之法，志存高远，后博览秦汉以来篆隶之道，无所不工，推陈出新，自成一家。王羲之的书法影响深远，被尊为"书圣"。唐太宗评曰："心慕手追，此人而已，其余区区之类，何足论哉！"

文化剪影　Cultural Outline

Wang Xizhi was of noble birth, whose family was on the same footing as the royal family of Sima. He was slow in speech as a child, but as an adult, he was good at thinking and known for his straightness. His fondness of calligraphy and the strong calligraphic atmosphere his family made him learn widely from others' strong points and became **proficient**① in official, **cursive**②, regular and running **scripts**③; breaking from the calligraphic style of Han and Wei, he created a brand-new calligraphy, varied but peaceful and natural in structure and exquisite but firm and powerful in handwriting. His calligraphy was described by later generations as "natural in nature" "floating like a cloud, vigorous like a startling dragon".

王羲之出身名门望族,其家族与皇族司马氏平起平坐。王羲之少时不善言辞,成人后却善于思辨,以刚直著称。他酷爱书法,家族书法氛围浓厚,他博采众长,精通隶、草、楷、行诸体,脱胎于汉魏书风,创造了全新的书法风格,字体结构多变而又平和自然,笔势细腻却又不失刚健。后人形容其书法"天质自然""飘若游云,矫若惊龙"。

Wang Xizhi excelled in various forms of calligraphy, in particular the running and regular scripts. His works of regular script consisted of *Huangting* **Sutra**④, *On Yue Yi* and *Cao E Stele*, which have produced profound influence on later generations; his works of running script contained *Post to the Maternal Aunt*, *Post of the Funeral Disturbance*, *Post of Health*, and *A Sketch of the Gathering at Orchid Arbor* has been highly praised by the calligraphers of the dynasties that followed, honored as "the best running script in the world" by Mi Fu, a great calligrapher of the Yuan Dynasty.

王羲之精通各种书体，尤擅行楷。其楷书作品有《黄庭经》《乐毅论》和《曹娥碑》，对后代影响深远；行书作品包括《姨母帖》《丧乱帖》《平安帖》和为历代书法家推崇备至的《兰亭集序》，被元代书法大家米芾誉为"天下第一行书"。

Behind Wang Xizhi's handwriting, there are quite a few stories about idioms left behind such as "having forceful strokes" "high mountains and lofty hills" "a **beneficent**⑤ breeze is graciously blowing", and so on. "Having forceful strokes" denotes that when he was seven years old, Wang Xizhi wrote some congratulatory words for the emperor on the wooden board for a carpenter to carve. The carpenter cut many times before he could see the bottom of inkblot. He marveled at Wang Xizhi's powerful handwriting. The idiom later describes one's profound comment or observations. The following idioms all derived from his *A Sketch of the Gathering at Orchid Arbor*, showing that in addition to the pursuit of perfect calligraphy, he also had extraordinary **attainments**⑥ in literature.

王羲之的书法背后，留下了不少成语故事，比如"入木三分""崇山峻岭""惠风和畅"等。"入木三分"讲的是王羲之七岁时为皇帝祝词,写在木板上让木匠师傅雕刻,木工削了半天木头才见墨迹的底部,惊叹王羲之笔力强劲,该成语后来比喻见解深刻。后边几个成语均出自王羲之的《兰亭集序》,说明他除了追求尽善尽美的书法艺术,在文学上也有非凡的造诣。

佳句点睛　Punchlines

1. All the virtuous come to meet here, the youth as well as the elder.

群贤毕至,少长咸集。

2. A breeze keeps the spring sun forever; the waters reflect the **twilight**① mountain clear.

风和春日永,水映暮山清。

3. The quiet orchids nestle among tall bamboos; the running water embraces the spring mountains.

幽兰间修竹,流水抱春山。

情景对话　Situational Dialogue

A: How many styles of Chinese calligraphy?

B: Generally, it can be classified into five styles: seal script, official script, cursive script, regular script and running script.

A: If I want to learn it, which style should I learn?

B: Regular script.

A: Why?

B: Because regular script is the most standard, easy to learn and grasp, and naturally regarded as calligraphic ABC.

A: What calligrapher shall I start from then?

B: The charm of learning calligraphy lies not only in itself. Have you heard about the story of Wang Xizhi?

A: Yes, I have. He was honored as the "sage of Chinese calligraphy".

B: Wonderful. His art of calligraphy has been described as "floating as a cloud and vigorous as a startling dragon". He has been honored as the spokesman for perfection.

A: How did he reach that summit?

B: It has a long story. In a word, he was able to learn from many masters and **expert**⑧ in integrating the strengths of many masters, which was an **indispensable**⑨ part of his success.

A: 中国书法有几种风格?

B: 一般来说,可以分为篆书、隶书、草书、楷书和行书五种。

A: 如果我想学,应该从哪种书法开始?

B: 楷书。

A: 为什么?

B: 因为楷书最规范,容易学也好掌握,自然被当成书法的入门字体。

A：那从哪位书法家开始学为好呢？

B：其实，学书法的魅力不仅在于书法本身。你听说过王羲之的故事吗？

A：听说过，他被誉为"书圣"。

B：他的书法艺术被喻为"飘若游云，矫若惊龙"，他还被当成尽善尽美的代言人。

A：他是怎么达到那种崇高境界的呢？

B：说来话长。总之，他能够师从多端，善于融多家之长，这是他成功不可或缺的重要一环。

生词注解 Notes

① proficient /prəˈfɪʃnt/ *adj.* 精通的；娴熟的

② cursive /ˈkɜːsɪv/ *adj.* 草书的；连笔的

③ script /skrɪpt/ *n.* 笔迹；剧本

④ sutra /ˈsuːtrə/ *n.* (梵文的或佛教的)经；箴言

⑤ beneficent /bɪˈnefɪsnt/ *adj.* 有裨益的；慈善的

⑥ attainment /əˈteɪnmənt/ *n.* 造诣；成就

⑦ twilight /ˈtwaɪlaɪt/ *adj.* 暮色的；黄昏的

⑧ expert /ˈekspɜːt/ *adj.* 专家的；内行的

⑨ indispensable /ˌɪndɪˈspensəbl/ *adj.* 不可缺少的；绝不可少的

顾恺之

Gu Kaizhi

导入语 Lead-in

顾恺之(348~409),字长康,晋陵无锡(今江苏无锡)人。东晋著名画家、绘画理论家和诗人。博学多闻,性诙谐,人多爱亲近之。工诗赋,曾作《筝赋》,自比嵇康之琴。尤擅丹青,描绘精妙,谢安赞曰:"有苍生以来未之有。"他精于人像、佛像、禽兽、山水等,以形写神,《魏晋胜流画赞》《论画》和《画云台山记》三篇画论为中国传统绘画的发展奠定了坚实的基础。其代表作有《洛神赋图》《女史箴图》《斫琴图》等。他被尊称为"中国画祖"和"山水画祖"。

文化剪影 Cultural Outline

Gu Kaizhi was highly accomplished in both drawing and literature. As a master of painting, he was good at drawing historical figures, Buddhist and Taoist portraits, mountains and waters, and fowls and beasts. His paintings of birds and animals inherited the style of Han, reflecting the development of tradition, and his figures of Buddhism and Taoism were both popular themes, mirroring people's beliefs then. In figure painting, he proposed to be lifelike and concentrated on the finishing touch of painting; his drawing line was thorough and **incessant**[①] like a spring silkworm spinning silk. Gu Kaizhi was one of the "Four Masters of the Six Dynasties", known as the "Ancestor of Traditional Chinese Painting".

顾恺之在绘画和文学方面皆有很高的造诣。作为丹青妙手,顾恺之精通历史人物、佛道肖像和山水禽兽。其飞禽走兽承汉代画风,反映传统发展,佛道画像皆为当代流行题材,反映时人的信仰。人物画主张传神勾勒,注重点睛之笔,笔迹周密,如春蚕吐丝,连绵不断。顾恺之是"六朝四大家"之一,被誉为"中国画祖"。

Gu Kaizhi created the density-style painting, whose lines are tight, vigorous and incessant, like spring silkworms spinning silk, spring clouds floating in the air and flowing water moving on the earth, natural and smooth, very suitable to embody the silk dress of the painted figures. He also made outstanding achievements in the theory of painting, putting forward the viewpoints such as theory of lifelikeness, which has made a far-reaching influence on later generations. Gu Kaizhi created quite a lot of paintings but few of them are in existence. His masterpieces included *The Court Ladies' **Admonitions**②, Painting of Ode to Goddess Luo River*, *Painting of Zhuoqin*, and so on.

顾恺之首创密体画,其线条紧劲连绵,如春蚕吐丝,春云浮空,流水行地,自然流畅,非常适合体现人物的丝绸服饰。他的画论也成就突出,提出了传神论等观点,对后世影响深远。顾恺之画作很多,但留存甚少,代表作有《女史箴图》《洛神赋图》《斫琴图》等。

Gu Kaizhi had "three wonders" in literature, painting and **infatuation**③. His literary wonder consisted in *Praising the Famous Paintings of Wei and Jin*, reviewed twenty-one masterpieces of Wei and Jin, including myths and legends, historical figures, religious stories, mountains and rivers, animals and beasts, and designed a series of painting and criticism standards, which set a model for Chinese painting theory. His painting wonder embodied in his *Paintings of the Ode on Goddess Luo River*, which depicted the love story between Cao Zhi and Goddess Luo River; it was **circuitous**④ and **meticulous**⑤ in depiction but distinct in layout, honored as one of the top ten traditional Chinese paintings. His wonder of infatuation was in wisdom.

顾恺之有文、画、痴"三绝"。其文字之"绝"在《魏晋胜流画赞》,该作评述了魏晋时期二十一幅名作,涉及神话传说、历史人物、宗教故事和山水禽兽，设计了一系列作画和评判标准，为中国画论树立典范。画作之"绝"体现在《洛神赋图》，该作品描绘曹植和洛神的爱情故事，画面曲折细致而又层次分明，被誉为中国十大传统名画之一。痴迷之"绝"在智慧。

佳句点睛 Punchlines

1. When the mountain falls and the sea runs dry, where will the fish and birds rely on?

山崩溟海竭，鱼鸟将何依？

2. The spring water fills the lakes and rivers, the summer clouds are full of fantastic mountain peaks, the autumn moon brightly shines, and the winter mountains are graced with solitary pines.

春水满泗泽，夏云多奇峰，秋月扬清辉，冬岭秀孤松。

3. Others ate sugarcane, starting from the sweetest part, threw it away when not sweet, but Gu did it from the end, and the more he ate, the sweeter he felt, in this way he was getting more and more enjoyable.

别人吃甘蔗从最甜处开始，不甜就扔掉，而顾恺之吃甘蔗从末梢吃起，越吃越甜，渐入佳境。

情景对话 Situational Dialogue

A: What I will never forget is his "three infatuations".

B: "Three infatuations"?

A: Namely, of painting, calculating and wisdom. One story says Gu Kaizhi did see his mother, and he repeatedly asked his father and painted his mother again and again. He did not stop painting until his father lit up and said, "It is exactly the same".

B: I read the story. No such infatuation could Gu Kaizhi rarely be a great painter. I also know his story of wisdom; it said Gu Kaizhi ate sugarcane from the end, reflecting his preference for a better and better life. I just wonder what you mean by the infatuation of calculating.

A: Gu Kaizhi was **obsessed**⑥ with small magic. Huan Xuan, a powerful minister, deceived him by giving a willow leaf, claiming it could make him invisible. The moment Gu Kaizhi took it, Huan Xuan peed against him and said the magic leaf made its presence so that he could not see Gu Kaizhi. Gu, however, actually accepted it to be true and took the leaf as priceless.

B: That was also a wise move to protect himself.

A: His infatuation means he was good at playing the fool.

B: In that case, Gu Kaizhi was not of small cleverness but of great wisdom.

A: Yes. What I really want to say is my "three sighs".

B: Tell me what the they are quickly.

A: The first sigh one is that wise men have to be silly. The second is that Gu Kaizhi's got quite a lot of good works but just a few remained and all are copies. And the third is that even the copy of *The Court Ladies' Admonitions* can only be found in the British Museum in London.

B: To lag behind is to be beaten. We should all strive to be strong and never to be **trampled**① upon at will.

A: 我难忘的是他的"三痴"。

B: "三痴"?

A: 就是痴画、痴算、痴智。有故事说,顾恺之从未见过母亲,他就反复询问父亲,反复画母亲的肖像,直到父亲双眼放光,说"像极了"才罢手。

B: 我看过这个故事。没有这种痴,顾恺之也难成大画家。那个"痴智"的故事我也知道,就是顾恺之倒吃甘蔗,反映其偏爱越来越好的生活。只是你说的"痴算"是什么呢?

A: 顾恺之痴迷小法术,权臣桓玄就欺骗他,给一片柳叶,称之能隐身。顾恺之刚一拿到,桓玄便冲他撒尿,说法宝显灵,他已看不见顾恺之。但是,顾竟信以为真,把柳叶视为至宝。

B: 那也是明哲保身之举。

A: 他的"痴算"就是善于装疯卖傻。

B: 这么说来,顾恺之不是小聪明,而是大智慧了。

A: 是的。不过我自己也有"三叹"。

B: 快说说是哪"三叹"?

A: 一叹聪明人也得当傻子。二叹顾恺之佳作甚多,但留存不多,皆为摹本。三叹《女史箴图》的摹本也只能在伦敦的大英博物馆里找到。

B: 落后就要挨打。我们都要奋发图强,绝不能再任人宰割。

生词注解　Notes

① incessant /ɪnˈsesnt/　*adj.* 连绵不绝的;持续不断的

② admonish /ədˈmɒnɪʃ/　*vt.* 告诫;警告

③ infatuation /ɪnˌfætʃuˈeɪʃn/　*n.* 痴迷;热恋

④ circuitous /səˈkjuːɪtəs/　*adj.* 曲折的;迂回的

⑤ meticulous /məˈtɪkjələs/　*adj.* 小心翼翼的;细心的

⑥ obsessed /əbˈsest/　*adj.* 痴迷的;念念不忘的

⑦ trample /ˈtræmpl/　*vi.* 践踏;踩碎

吴道子

Wu Daozi

导入语 Lead-in

吴道子(约680～759),又名道玄,阳翟(今河南禹州)人。唐代著名画家,被尊称为"画圣"。少年孤苦贫寒,曾游学洛阳,师从张旭和贺知章,书法不成,改学绘画,刻苦好学,悟性非凡,未及弱冠便"穷丹青之妙"。曾做小吏数年,后浪迹东洛,以绘画为生。随着画名日盛,开元初年被征召入宫,任内教博士,"非有诏不得画",常从唐玄宗巡游作画,长于壁画,尤擅佛道像和人物画。晚年受诏再次入蜀作画。其主要作品有《送子天王图》《明皇受篆图》《十指钟馗图》等。苏轼评价说:"道子画人物,如以灯取影,逆来顺往,旁见侧出。横斜平直,各相乘除,得自然之数,不差毫末。出新意于法度之中,寄妙理于豪放之外,所谓游刃余地,运斤成风,盖古今一人而已。"

文化剪影 Cultural Outline

Wu Daozi was largely occupied in religious murals which were of abundant themes and of a far-reaching influence. According to the record, in the Buddhist and Taoist temples in Chang'an and Luoyang, Wu Daozhi painted over three hundred **frescoes**①, various in postures and different from one another. He was also good at landscape painting, enjoying a high reputation. He once **escorted**② Emperor Xuanzong of Tang to travel to Luoyang and came across General Pei Min and Calligrapher Zhang Xu. They performed together; Pei contributed a sword dance to music, Zhang dedicated a wall of cursive script and Wu Daozhi presented a painting in an instant, who became famous across the East Capital for a time, later honored as the "Sage of Sword", the "Sage of Cursive Script" and the "Sage of Painting".

吴道子主要从事宗教壁画创作,其作品主题丰富,影响深远。据记载,吴道子曾在长安、洛阳两地寺庙道观中,绘制壁画多达三百余幅,姿态万千,各不相同。吴道子在工山水方面同样赫赫有名。一次,他随唐玄宗游洛阳,逢将军裴旻和书法家张旭,于是同台献艺,裴旻舞剑一曲,张旭草书一壁,道玄顷刻一画,一时誉满东都,三人后被称为"剑圣""草圣"和"画圣"。

Wu Daozi's painting skills were outstanding, bold, innovative and **unconventional**③. His paintings were known as "Wu's Model" and his painting style had been imitated and referenced by many painters after the Tang Dynasty. In religious murals there were *Tota King*, *Peacock Ming King* and *Ten-finger Zhong Kui*, and so on. In landscape painting there were paintings of *The Nanyue Mountains*, *The Double Forests*, *Donkeys* and so on, whose masterpiece was *The Three-hundred-li Landscape of the Jialing River*, which was completed within one day, revealing the lovely scenery on both banks to the greatest extent.

吴道子绘画技艺卓然超群,大胆创新,不落俗套,其绘画作品被称之为"吴家样",画风为唐代以后诸多画家效仿和借鉴。吴道子的宗教壁画有《托塔天王图》《孔雀明王图》《十指钟馗图》等,山水画有《南岳图》《双林图》《群驴图》等,代表作《嘉陵江山水三百里图》一日而就,尽现两岸旖旎风光。

Wu Daozi was an **omnipotent**④ painter. In terms of techniques, he created "Orchid Leaf Skill", which made use of a style like an orchid leaf or water shield to manifest **pleats**⑤. Of the painted figures, their sleeves and ribbons were all lively and vigorous, like whirling about in the wind, described as "Belts Like Being Blown by Wind". In terms of speed, he often accomplished it in one stroke. According to the legend, he was drawing the Door-God of at Longxing Temple, when audiences were crowded. When he **wielded**⑥ his long brush, it turned like wind or lightning. At that moment, the immortal had a full moon and golden light over his head. The crowd cheered and the cheers shook the whole street.

吴道子是一位全能画家。就技法而言,吴道子创造了"兰叶描",利用状如兰叶或莼菜一样的笔法表现衣褶。所画人物的衣袖、飘带皆生动灵现,有迎风飘舞之状,被形容为"吴带当风"。就速度而言,吴道子作画经常一蹴而就。传说他在龙兴寺画门神的,观众如堵,只见他长笔一挥,如风过电转,霎时神仙头顶一轮圆月金光。人群欢呼,惊动了整个街道。

佳句点睛　Punchlines

1. Wu Daozi was mainly engaged in the creation of religious murals which were of abundant themes and far-reaching influence.

吴道子主要从事宗教壁画创作,其作品主题丰富,影响深远。

2. There were "three sages" in the Tang Dynasty; one of them was Wu Daozi, sage of painting.

唐朝有"三圣",其中之一就是画圣吴道子。

3. Li Sixun's work of several months and Wu Daoxuan's of one day were both extremely wonderful.

李思训数月之功,吴道玄一日之迹,皆极其妙也。

情景对话 Situational Dialogue

A: There are "three sages" in the Tang dynasty. Do you know who they are?

B: They are sages of poetry, cursive script and painting.

A: Then, what is your impression of Wu Daoxuan?

B: You mean Wu Daozi, the sage of painting? I identify him with the title of painting sage. I feel his greatness resulted from two kinds of "fusion". First, he mixed painting with calligraphy and sword dancing. Second, he fused folk style and court style. Wu Daozi became famous in the countryside, and then was recruited into the court where he also enjoyed a high reputation, and eventually returned to be folk painter, who could only paint without a signature.

A: Yes. Because of his generous teachings in the court, he had many famous academic learners. Though an **anonymous**[①] painter in his late years, he spread techniques among the folk painters.

B: It's perhaps his concentration just on arts that made his popularity with both academic and folk schools of painting.

A: What I want to say is that he got another two "mixtures".

B: Go ahead.

A: One is the combination of religious art with his Wu's model. Under his brush, there were not only lively Buddhist figures but also impressive Taoist portraits, which is a kind of cultural integration. The other is between self and the times; he could hide himself into the historical period, regardless of its ups and downs. The anonymous paintings like *The King of Heaven Sending a Son* can be an illustration.

B: In this case, there should be more fusion. Wu Daozi lived in the Kaiyuan Flourishing Age, when there must be lots of cultural exchanges.

A: 唐朝有"三圣"。你知道都是谁吗?

B: 他们是诗圣、草圣和画圣。

A: 那你对吴道玄有什么印象?

B: 你是说"画圣"吴道子吧?我认同他的"画圣"称号。我觉得其成功源自两个"融合"。首先,是他的绘画融入了书法和剑舞,其次,融合了民间画和宫廷画。吴道子出身乡野,后应诏入宫,享有盛誉,最终回归民间,只能默默作画。

A: 是的。因其在宫中不吝赐教,他拥有不少著名的学院派学生。尽管他晚年是一无名画师,却在民间画工中传播技艺。

B: 或许,正是由于他只专注艺术,才能在民间画派和学院画派中雨露均沾。

A: 他还有两个"结合"。

B: 你说。

A: 一个是宗教艺术和"吴家样"的结合。其画笔下,不仅有生机勃勃的佛像,道像也令人印象深刻。另一个是在自身和时代之间,他能够隐身于历史,无所谓上下浮沉。比如无名之作《天王送子图》就是例证。

B: 既然如此,一定还有更多融合。吴道子生在开元盛世,肯定有许多文化交流活动。

生词注解 Notes

① fresco /ˈfreskəʊ/　*n.* 壁画;湿壁画

② escort /ɪˈskɔːt/　*vt.* 护卫;护送

③ unconventional /ˌʌnkənˈvenʃnl/　*adj.* 不因循守旧的;新奇的

④ omnipotent /ɒmˈnɪpətənt/　*adj.* 无所不能的;万能的

⑤ pleat /pliːt/　*n.*(布料上缝的)褶

⑥ wield /wiːld/　*vt.* 挥;使用(武器、工具等)

⑦ anonymous /əˈnɒnɪməs/　*adj.* 不知姓名的;匿名的

齐白石

Qi Baishi

  导入语 Lead-in

齐白石(1864~1957),本名纯芝,字渭青,号兰亭,后改名璜,号众多,最有名的是白石。祖籍安徽宿州砀山,生于湖南长沙府湘潭(今湖南湘潭)。近现代中国绘画大师。齐白石自幼喜画,早年拜师学雕花木工,自学花鸟人物,后拜师学诗文、画肖像养家,三十岁建诗社,吟诗作画、摹刻金石,后游历多地,结交名士,饱览诸多名家真迹,五十五岁定居北京,辗转教学,有《白石诗草》《借山吟馆诗草》问世。新中国成立后,获"人民艺术家"称号。代表作有《蛙声十里出山泉》《墨虾》《山水十二条屏》等。齐白石弟子众多,其中包括李苦禅、李可染、梅兰芳、新凤霞等。

文化剪影　Cultural Outline

In his life, Qi Baishi was in pursuit of painting, literature and stone carving, with a road full of ups and downs but enjoying various reputations. He was versed in painting flowers, birds, insects, fish, landscape and figures, sometimes with full and delightful ink in a flowing and **lucid**[①] style, sometimes with bright color, **scrupulous**[②] about every detail, sometimes with a bizarre conception, rich in creation, it completely followed nature to seek vigor of life. His painting, poems, calligraphy and seals are known as the "four wonders".

齐白石一生求画、求文、求金石，道路坎坷，享誉众多。他擅长画花鸟虫鱼和山水人物，或笔墨饱满、酣畅淋漓，或色彩明快、一丝不苟，或构思奇异、富于创造，但均道法自然，求生机一片。他的绘画、诗文、书法和印章被誉为"四绝"。

Qi Baishi was diligent in his life; he made more than thirty thousand paintings, over three thousand poems and quite a few volumes of autobiography and manuscripts. He was very good at drawing fish and shrimps. He preferred shrimps most; his love for and painting of shrimps is a story passed on with approval in the art circles. He played with shrimps as a boy and learned to paint them as a youth. In his forties he imitated shrimp drawings from the painters of Ming and Qing such as Xu Wei and Li Futang. At the age of sixty-three, he still felt that his shrimps were not similar enough in appearance, so he bought and raised shrimps at home, put them on the desk, observed them each day, and finally entered the realm of **transformation**[③]. Shrimps had become one of his art symbols as well.

齐白石一生勤勉,留有三万余幅画作,三千余首诗词、自述及文稿手迹多卷。他擅画鱼虾,对虾青睐有加;他爱虾、画虾是画坛美谈。齐白石少时钓虾玩,青年学画虾;不惑之年临摹虾画,向徐渭、李复堂等明清画家求经。六十三岁时画虾已达形似,犹觉不够生气,便买虾养虾,置于案头,每日观察,终入化境,虾也成了他的艺术符号之一。

Qi Baishi's artistic features are embodied in two kinds of life. The first is strong local flavor, simple farmer consciousness and childlike innocence, which is called "inner life". The second is the sprightly and **ardent**[④] color, sharp contrast in ink, simple and honest images and composition with oddness in evenness, which is called "external life". Two kinds of life depend on each other and evolve each other, forming the artistic image and value pursuit of the circle of life.

齐白石的艺术特色体现了两种生命力。一是浓厚的乡土气息、淳朴的农民意识和天真烂漫的童心,世人称之为"内在生命"。二是明快热烈的色彩,强烈对比的墨色,浑朴稚拙的造型,平正见奇的构成,世人称之为"外在生命"。两种生命相互依存、相互演化,形成了生生不息的艺术形象和价值追求。

佳句点睛 Punchlines

1. Qi Baishi did not paint the fish in ink, but he made people see long rivers and swimming fish.

齐白石画的鱼儿没有上色,却能让人看到长河与游鱼。

2. The beauty of painting lies between likeness and unlikeness, for too much likeness appeals to vulgarity, but unlikeness **deceives**⑤ the world.

绘画妙在似与不似之间,太似为媚俗,不似为欺世。

3. He who learns from me will live while he who imitates me will die. Neither talk about others' disadvantages nor your advantages. Smile when **abused**⑥ or praised.

学我者生,似我者死。勿道人之短,勿说己之长。人骂之一笑,人誉之一笑。

情景对话 Situational Dialogue

A: What shall we chat about today?

B: We might as well chat about Qi Baishi, the people's artist. He learned by himself, starting as a carpenter. He eventually became famous in art circles for the "Four Wonders", namely, painting, seal engraving, calligraphy and poems.

A: His paintings are full of sound and color, well-known at home and abroad. I remember that a European celebrity commented, "Qi Baishi did not paint the fish in ink, but he made people see long rivers and swimming fish."

B: What you said is Picasso. It's said that when Zhang Daqian invited him to China, he said, "I dare not go there, because you have a Qi Baishi there."

A: Can you tell me something about his works?

B: Yes, I can. He was expert in painting **aquatic**[7] animals, such as *Ink Shrimps* and *The Croaking of Frogs Ten Li out of a Mountain Spring*.

A: Right. Shrimp is an art symbol of Qi Baishi.

B: But I think the latter is more distinctive. In the painting there is a black valley, in its middle a gurgling stream, where there are six tadpoles swimming down, and in the distance are several dots of hilltops, making people in the infinite **reverie**[8] of the future.

A: There are really poems, paintings and dreams.

B: Well said.

A: 今天聊什么呢？

B: 不妨聊聊齐白石这位人民艺术家。他是木匠起家，自学成才，终于修成正果，以画印书诗"四绝"闻名。

A: 他的画作有声有色，在国内外享有盛誉。记得欧洲有位名人评价说："齐白石画的鱼儿没有上色,却使人看到长河与游鱼。"

B：是毕加索说的。据说张大千邀请他来中国时,他说："我可不敢去那里,因为你们有个齐白石。"

A：那你能介绍一下他的作品吗？

B：能。他最拿手的是画水中生灵,如《墨虾》和《蛙声十里出山泉》。

A：对。虾是齐白石的一个艺术标志。

B：不过,我认为那幅《蛙声十里出山泉》更有特色。画里一条黑峡谷,中间是叮咚的山泉,里边六只蝌蚪顺流而下,远处点了几个山头,让人沉浸在对未来的无限遐想之中。

A：真是有诗、有画、有梦想。

B：说得好。

生词注解 Notes

① lucid /ˈluːsɪd/ *adj.* 表达清楚的；头脑清醒的

② scrupulous /ˈskruːpjələs/ *adj.* 一丝不苟的；恪守道德规范的

③ transformation /ˌtrænsfəˈmeɪʃn/ *n.* (彻底的)变化；转变

④ ardent /ˈɑːdnt/ *adj.* 热烈的；激情的

⑤ deceive /dɪˈsiːv/ *vt.* 欺骗；诓骗

⑥ abuse /əˈbjuːs/ *vt.* 妄用；滥用

⑦ aquatic /əˈkwætɪk/ *adj.* 水生的；水上的

⑧ reverie /ˈrevəri/ *n.* 幻想；梦想

徐悲鸿

Xu Beihong

导入语 Lead-in

徐悲鸿(1895~1953)，本名许寿康，江苏宜兴人。中国现当代著名画家、美术教育家。他出身平民，六岁习文，九岁作画，十三岁随父辗转乡里卖画为生。二十岁重游上海，入震旦大学攻法语，得康有为支持，书画并进。二十四岁留学巴黎，专攻西洋美术。三十二岁归国，投身美术教育。新中国成立

后，当选全国政协代表，任中央美院院长，笔耕不辍。其代表作有《奔马图》《八骏图》《群马》《愚公移山图》《田横五百士》等。徐悲鸿被誉为中国百年艺术史上的"丹青巨擘、教育巨子"。

文化剪影 Cultural Outline

As a boy, Xu Beihong learned and drew from his father, wandering and struggling for a living. During his study in Shanghai, he accepted the **concept**① of realistic painting from the masters like Wu Daozi, Li Cheng and Fan Kuan, and went after the style of democracy and science due to the New Culture Movement. During his stay in Europe, he inherited its classical style of painting. After returning to his motherland, he took part in the "Nanguo Society" organized by Tian Han and Ouyang Yuqian, **advocating**② "to seek truth first before beauty and goodness".

徐悲鸿幼时随父亲学画,为生活辗转奔波。在上海求学期间,他受到吴道子、李成、范宽等大师的写实绘画理念的熏陶,又因新文化运动而追求民主科学之风。旅欧期间,他继承了欧洲古典主义画风。学成归国后,参与田汉、欧阳予倩组织的"南国社",倡导"求美、求善之前先得求真"。

Xu Beihong combined the East and the West, created a lot in his life, with more than one thousand works in existence. His representative works consisted of *The Old Woman*, *Tian Heng and His Five Hundred Warriors*, *Horses*, *The **Galloping**③ Horse*, *The Foolish Man Removing the Mountains*, and so on, which carried forward realism and reflected the idea of the people, making his oil paintings, Chinese paintings and sketches into a new realm.

徐悲鸿的作品东西合璧,一生创作甚多,有一千多件作品留存于世。其代表作有《老妇》《田横五百士》《群马》《奔马》《愚公移山》等,他的画作弘扬现实主义,体现人民思想,使油画、中国画和素描进入了新境界。

Xu Beihong developed his own school in the history of the Chinese painting. He was good at sketching, oil painting and traditional Chinese painting and often integrated the three of them with the historical culture. He created a wide range of subjects, such as mountains and waters, birds and flowers, running beasts, figures, history and mythology, all lifelike, **vibrant**④, energetic, full of fighting spirit. Taking the example of *Tian Heng and His Five Hundred Warriors*, it was full of patriotism and humanism, showing the Chinese nation's **indomitable**⑤ power and reflecting the nation's anxiety and indignation and desire for light. His paintings of galloping horses are, in particular, well-known in the world and have become the symbol of modern Chinese painting.

徐悲鸿在中国绘画史上独树一帜。他擅长素描、油画和中国画,常融三技和历史文化于一体。他的创作题材十分广泛,包含山水、花鸟、走兽、人物、历史、神话,所画无不栩栩如生,生机勃勃,充满活力与斗志。以《田横五百士》为例,画中充满爱国主义和人文主义,表现出中华民族的威武不屈,反映出民族的忧愤情绪和对光明的渴望。其奔马画作更是享誉世界,成为现代中国画的象征。

佳句点睛　Punchlines

1. A person cannot be **arrogant**[6], but not without **loftiness**[7].

人不可有傲气，但不可无傲骨。

2. Love is precious because it cannot be replaced.

爱情之所以宝贵，是因为它不能被替代。

3. Everyone's life should leave something noble and useful for future generations.

每个人的一生都应该给后代留下一些高尚有益的东西。

情景对话　Situational Dialogue

A: "A person cannot be arrogant, but not without loftiness." Do you know who said it?

B: Xu Beihong.

A: Do you know why he said that?

B: No, I don't.

A: Xu Beihong had some experience of studying abroad. When he studied in Paris, a foreign classmate looked down on China and often **degraded**[8] China by saying some insulting words against the Chinese people. Mr. Xu told him, "Since you despise my country, from now on I represent my country and you represent yours and we'll see it when we graduate."

B: What happened then?

A: Xu Beihong wrote that line to inspire himself. Four years later, his paintings could be compared with the contemporary artists in the West; and after another four years in Europe, he developed his own painting idea and style.

B: It seems that there's surely a story behind every shiny word.

A: He stuck to this belief throughout his later creating career. He always integrated historical themes into his paintings. During the Anti-Japanese War, he contributed a lot against the Japanese invaders. And after the founding of new China, he created many works to sing the new life of the people.

B: He did keep pace with the times, encouraging the people to struggle and move on ever.

A: Yes, he did. That's what he called "something noble and beneficial".

B: You're right.

A:"人不可有傲气,但不可无傲骨。"你知道这句话是谁说的吗?

B: 徐悲鸿。

A: 你知道他为什么说那句话吗?

B: 不知道。

A: 徐悲鸿有过一段留学经历。他在巴黎学习时,一名外国同班同学瞧不起中国,经常说些侮辱中国人的话来贬低中国。徐先生就对他说:"既然你瞧不起我的国家,那好,从现在开始,我代表我的国家,你代表你的国家,我们等到毕业的时候再看彼此的成果。"

B: 然后呢?

A: 然后徐悲鸿就写下那句话激励自己。四年后,徐悲鸿的绘画可以跟西方同时代的画家相媲美了。在欧洲又漂泊了四年之后,他形成了自己的绘画思想和风格。

B: 看来闪光的话语背后必有故事。

A: 是的。这种信念贯穿了其后的创作生涯。他总是不断地融历史事实到自己画作当中。抗战期间,他贡献了许多作品以反抗日本侵略者。新中国成立后,他又创造了许多作品来歌颂人民的新生活。

B: 他的确是与时俱进,一直在鼓舞人民永远奋斗向前。

A: 这就是他所谓的"高尚有益的东西"吧。

B: 说得没错。

生词注解 Notes

① concept /ˈkɒnsept/ *n.* 概念;观念

② advocate /ˈædvəkeɪt/ *vt.* 提倡;拥护

③ gallop /ˈɡæləp/ *vi.* (马等)飞奔;疾驰

④ realm /relm/ *n.* 王国;领域

⑤ indomitable /ɪnˈdɒmɪtəbl/ *adj.* 不屈不挠的；毫不气馁的

⑥ arrogant /ˈærəgənt/ *adj.* 傲慢的；自大的

⑦ loftiness /ˈlɒftɪnəs/ *n.* 高傲；崇高

⑧ degrade /dɪˈgreɪd/ *vt.* 侮辱；使……受屈辱

张大千

Chang Dai-Chien

导入语 Lead-in

张大千(1899～1983),本名张正权,字季爱,号大千,四川内江人,现当代著名泼墨画家、书法家。生于书香门第,十八岁留学日本,自学诗画治印,二十岁回国,首次个人画展便一鸣惊人,百幅作品顷刻售罄,开始卖画为生。三十岁识徐悲鸿,后成立正社书画会,参加法国画展,任中央大学教授,办画展、出画集。五十岁后漂泊世界,办巡回书画展,被西方文坛誉为"东方之笔",又被称为"临摹天下名画最多的画家"。他是二十世纪中国画坛最具传奇色彩的泼墨画工,尤其在山水画方面成就非凡。

文化剪影   Cultural Outline

Chang Dai-Chien and his second elder brother Zhang Shanzi founded the "High Wind Hall School", which was legendary in the 20th-century Chinese painting. Chang Dai-Chien long admired Zhang Dafeng, who was good at poetry, literature, calligraphy and painting in the early Qing Dynasty. Zhang Shanzi looked up to Liu Bang, Emperor Gaozu of Han, and took interest in the two characters of "High Wind" in Liu Bang's *Song of High Wind*. The brothers named their studio as High Wind Hall in Shanghai. Since his fifties, he moved overseas and held art exhibitions around the world, and he was elected one of the great contemporary painters by New York International Art Academy for his **Begonia**① shown in Paris. After his late sixties, dramatic changes underwent in his painting style in the late sixties, with the combination of splash-ink and splash-color. Since he moved to Taibei, his four volumes of *Chang Dai-Chien's Calligraphy and Painting Collection* have been published **successively**②.

张大千与其二哥张善子创立"大风堂派",在二十世纪的中国画坛颇富传奇色彩。张大千一向仰慕清初大画家张大风诗文书画之无所不精。张善子仰慕汉高祖刘邦,对《大风歌》的"大风"二字尤感兴趣。于是,兄弟俩在上海给画室命名"大风堂"。五十年代,张大千迁居国外办世界巡回画展,因在巴黎展出的《秋海棠》而被纽约国际艺术学会选为"当代伟大画家"。六十年代后期其画风大变,泼墨泼彩,迁居台北后有《张大千书画集》四卷先后问世。

Chang Dai-Chien was a **versatile**③ painter, whose most creative was the splash-color technique. His masterpiece *Ten-Thousand-Li Yangtze River* was a typical painting with splash-ink and splash-color. Technically, it adopted such techniques as breaking ink, **accumulating**④ ink and splashing ink and blended his individual splashing ink, making a style "with the combination of splashing and freehand brushwork and with the integration of ink and color". The painting is twenty meters long and over half a meter tall, magnificent in **layout**⑤, varied in scene but like nature itself.

张大千属全能型画家,其最具创新的是泼彩法。他的代表作《长江万里图》是一幅典型的泼墨泼彩画作,就技法而言,既采用了传统山水画的破墨、积墨和泼墨等技巧,又融入了个人的泼彩法,形成了"泼写兼施,色墨交融"的风格。该画作长达二十米,高超过半米,布局恢宏,气象万千却又浑然天成。

Chang Dai-Chien learned from the ancient, the current and nature, but he was not limited to that; he developed the splash-ink method, created splash-color and ink-color splashing techniques, and improved the character of the domestic Xuan Paper, Chinese art paper made in Xuancheng, Anhui Province. His imitation works look almost genuine; compared with the genuine works of the ancient masters, the artistic value of his **replication**⑥ has even gone beyond them. He traveled around China before fifty and after that he toured across the world. His accumulation of creative materials is so exhaustible that no other painters could match, which has formed the style of High Wind Hall School of "all flowers bloom together".

张大千师古人、师今人、师造化，但并不拘泥。他发展了泼墨法，创造了泼彩法和泼彩墨技艺，同时还改进了国产宣纸的质地。张大千的临摹作品几近乱真，与古代名家真品相比，其仿古作品的艺术价值有过之而无不及。他五十岁之前遍游祖国，五十岁之后周游世界，积累了取之不尽、用之不竭的创作素材，非其他画家所能比拟，形成了大风堂画派"百花齐放"的风格。

佳句点睛　Punchlines

1. Brushwork is difficult, inkwork is more difficult and washwork is the most difficult.

笔法难，墨法更难，水法极难。

2. A painter should learn from heaven and earth and stick not to one frame; the so-called nature is in hand.

画家当以天地为师，不可拘泥一格，所谓造化在手耶！

3. If you want to get rid of vulgarity, **fickleness**[7] and **triteness**[8] in art work, the first is to read, the second is to read more, and the third is to read systematically and selectively.

作画如欲脱俗气、洗浮气、除匠气,方法有三,第一是读书,第二是多读书,第三是须有系统、有选择地读书。

 情景对话 Situational Dialogue

A: Chang Dai-Chien was the creator of splash-ink technique. Do you know what his masterpiece is?

B: It's *The Ten Thousand-Li Yangtze River*. It is a typical painting with both splash-ink and splash-color techniques. This is his longest and even greatest work, and it is the culmination of his seventy years' painterly skills. Since then, he had not painted more than twenty meters.

A: Seventy years? I know he completed it within ten days.

B: That is what I want to say next. When making the piece, he was already seventy but still **energetic**① so he completed the great work quickly.

A: I see. You mean the great painting was based on his seventy-year painting experience.

B: Besides his excellent craftsmanship, I have something more discovered.

A: What is it?

B: What impressed me the most was that Chang Dai-Chien drifted abroad, but he must be thinking of China deep down. So I think that this work also represents his deep feelings for the motherland.

A: Yes. Chang Dai-Chien really wrote, "Half a lifetime only in my paintings I can draw the regions south of the Yangtze River, but I cannot return till now."

B: It was from the bottom of his heart.

A: 张大千是泼彩技法的创始人。你知道他的代表作是什么吗？

B: 是《长江万里图》，该作品采用了泼墨泼彩技艺。这是他最长的、甚至是最伟大的作品，是他七十年画工的结晶。从那时起，他就没有超过二十米的画作了。

A: 七十年？我知道他是在十日之内完成该幅作品的。

B: 那正是我要说的。绘制该幅作品时，他已年届七旬，但依然精力充沛，于是很快就完成了这幅大作。

A: 明白了。你是说，这幅巨作基于他七十年的绘画经历。

B: 除了他的杰出技艺，我还有更多的发现。

A: 是什么？

B: 我印象最深的是，尽管张大千飘零海外，但他内心深处一定在思念中国。所以，我认为这幅作品也代表他对祖国的深深思念。

A: 是啊！张大千确实写过："半世江南图画里，而今能画不能归。"

B: 这是他的肺腑之言。

生词注解 Notes

① begonia /bɪˈgəʊnɪə/ *n.* 秋海棠

② successively /səkˈsesɪvlɪ/　*adv.* 先后地；相继地

③ versatile /ˈvɜːsətaɪl/　*adj.* 多才多艺的；多面手的

④ accumulate /əˈkjuːmjəleɪt/　*vt.* 积累；堆积

⑤ layout /ˈleɪaʊt/　*n.* 布局；设计

⑥ replication /ˌreplɪˈkeɪʃn/　*n.* 复制；仿制

⑦ fickleness /ˈfɪklnəs/　*n.* 浮躁；变化无常

⑧ triteness /ˈtraɪtnəs/　*n.* 陈腐；平凡

⑨ energetic /ˌenəˈdʒetɪk/　*adj.* 精力充沛的；充满活力的

梅兰芳

Mei Lanfang

导入语 Lead-in

梅兰芳（1894~1961），本名梅澜，又名鹤鸣，字畹华，艺名兰芳，著名京剧表演艺术大师。民国时创演新戏二十余部，学昆曲，学绘画，鉴古玩，拍电影，访日美，获文学荣誉博士学位，创立梅派；抗战时蓄胡罢演，抗战胜利后重新登台。新中国成立后参加开国大典。六十五岁创编《穆桂英挂帅》，拍彩色电影《游园惊梦》。代表作有《贵妃醉酒》《打渔杀家》《宇宙锋》《天女散花》等。

杰出人物

文化剪影 Cultural Outline

As an artistic master of Beijing Opera, Mei Lanfang enjoyed a great reputation at home and abroad. Born in a family of opera artists, he was diligent, studious and constantly innovative all his life. He went deep into the traditional culture such as literature, painting, music, dance and costume, and blended them into the art of Beijing Opera. He **initiated**① and starred a large number of excellent operas and developed the unique Mei-style art.

作为京剧艺术大师,梅兰芳在国内外均享有盛誉。他出身梨园世家,一生勤勉好学,不断创新。他钻研文学、绘画、音乐、舞蹈和服饰等传统文化,并将其融入京剧艺术之中,创演了大量优秀剧目,形成了独树一帜的梅派艺术。

Mei Lanfang kept innovating all the time. His *Regrets of Life and Death* was the first color film of China, in which a series of innovations in singing voices, performances, lighting and make-up opened up a new realm in Beijing Opera. In his late years he created *Mu Guiying Taking Command*, **eulogizing**② the Yang's family, all faithful and upright and willing to share concerns for the country; it was of practical and instructive significance, reflecting Mei Lanfang's ideological realm and lofty artistic outlook, which should be loyal to the country and the people.

梅兰芳不断创新。他的《生死恨》是中国第一部彩色电影,一系列唱腔、表演、灯光、化妆等方面的革新开辟了京剧艺术的新境界。晚年他创编《穆桂英挂帅》,歌颂杨家将"一门忠良,为国分忧",具有现实意义和教育意义,体现出梅兰芳的思想境界和崇高的艺术观,即艺术要忠于祖国和人民。

Mei Lanfang had a distinctive artistic style. His **aria**③ was mellow, smooth and beautiful, rich in feelings. His performance was versed in taking advantages of singing, reciting, acting and fighting, showing luxury in simplicity, loveliness in **demureness**④ and generosity in attraction. His dance revealed the beauty of norm in every respect. His make-up was mixed with the southern style in accordance with facial features, which initiated the practice to make up female performers in the north. He pursued the innovation of drama theory. His innovation, the Mei-style Beijing Opera, is symbolic of Beijing opera, and also the living proof that Chinese opera stands out among the three major performing arts in the world.

梅兰芳的艺术风格独特,他的唱腔醇厚流丽,富含感情,表演善用唱念做打,于质朴中见华贵,于端庄中含俏丽,于妩媚中显大方。其舞蹈的最大特点就是均显程式化之美。化妆方面,他根据脸型,融南方风格,开北方旦角化妆之先河。梅兰芳追求戏剧理论创新。梅兰芳的创新——梅派京剧,是中国京剧的标志,也是中国戏剧屹立于世界三大表演艺术的活证。

 佳句点睛　Punchlines

1. A really good play is to break the rules.
真正的好戏是人打破规矩。

2. In addition to our regular work, we must also form the habit of regular rest.
我们在坚持工作之外,还必须养成坚持休息的习惯。

3. I'm a clumsy learner of art, without **sufficient**① genius but all by my hard work.
我是个拙笨的学艺者,没有充分的天才,全凭苦学。

 情景对话　Situational Dialogue

A: Do you know Mei Lanfang?

B: Mei Lanfang? Nobody doesn't know him, who was the first of the Four Major Female Roles in Beijing Opera.

A: He was honored as the "Most Beautiful Strivers of New China" last night.

B: That's an amazing honor. How did he get the title of "Most Beautiful Striver"?

A: This is just what I feel interested in. What does it suggest?

B: His great influence, of course. But besides the Four Great Female Roles led by him made Beijing Opera **flourish**⑥ and opened up the situation that "all flowers bloom together", what else is worth remembering?

A: He earned his fame in his life, but his great influence would be after he passed away.

B: Since that, he should be remembered not just for his *Drunken Beauty* or *Mu Guiying Taking Command*.

A: Yes. Besides his Mei-style art, his other stories should also be worth thinking and learning.

B: What has impressed me most is his constant innovation, integrating the advantages of various schools. He learned not only dramatic techniques like qingyi, huadan and lighting, but also non-dramatic skills; for example, he learned painting from Qi Baishi and eventually his performance is known as "Stage Landscape Painting".

A: Yeah. He said, "A really good play is to break the rules."

B: He was the first who used spotlights on stage and participated in making a color film in China.

A: During the Anti-Japanese War, he refused to perform for the invaders, telling the Japanese official, "Off stage, I'm a man."

B: He warned us, "Come to this world in costumes, not to stain the characters in the play."

A: What a real man of virtue and art!

B: He deserved to be "The Most Beautiful Striver".

杰出人物

A: 你知道梅兰芳吗?

B: 梅兰芳谁不知道?他可是京剧界的"四大名旦"之首。

A: 他昨晚为评为"新中国最美奋斗者"。

B: 那可是个了不起的荣誉。他是怎么获得"最美奋斗者"的呢?

A: 这正是我感兴趣的。这说明了什么?

B: 当然说明了他影响巨大。可是,除了他领衔的"四大名旦"让京剧走向兴盛,开创中国戏剧史上的"百花齐放"局面,还有什么是值得纪念的呢?

A: 他赢得名声在生前,但他的巨大影响在身后。

B: 如此说来,他被人记住的不仅仅是他的《贵妃醉酒》《穆桂英挂帅》。

A: 对。除了他的梅派艺术,他的其他故事也值得我们思考和学习。

B: 我印象最深的是他不断创新,融百家之长。不仅学习青衣、花旦、灯光等业内技艺,而且学习业外技能,比如他跟齐白石学绘画,其表演也被称为"舞台山水画"。

A: 对。他说过:"真正的好戏是人打破规矩。"

B: 他是第一个在舞台上使用追光灯的表演者,也是他参与拍摄了中国第一部彩色电影。

A: 抗战期间,他拒绝给侵略者演出;他告诉日本军官:"在台下,我是个男人。"

B: 他曾经告诫后人:"你穿着戏服到这世上,小心把戏里的人物给弄脏了。"

A: 真是德艺双馨啊!

B: 所以,他不愧为"最美奋斗者"。

生词注解　Notes

① initiate /ɪˈnɪʃɪeɪt/　*vt.* 创始;发起

② eulogize /ˈjuːlədʒaɪz/　*vt.* 颂扬;称赞

③ aria /ˈɑːrɪə/　*n.* 唱腔;(尤指歌剧或清唱剧中的)咏叹调

④ demureness /dɪˈmjʊə(r)nəs/　*n.* 端庄;娴静

⑤ sufficient /səˈfɪʃnt/　*adj.* 充分的;足够的

⑥ flourish /ˈflʌrɪʃ/　*vi.* 兴盛;繁荣

杰出人物

 # 李小龙

Bruce Lee

导入语 Lead-in

李小龙(1940~1973),本名李振藩,祖籍广东佛山,生于美国旧金山。著名武术家,表演艺术家,世界武道变革先驱,综合格斗和功夫电影开创人,截拳道创始人,中华武术首位全球推广人,好莱坞电影首位华人主角。李小龙自幼随父练习太极拳,十四岁师承咏春拳宗师叶问,练习百家拳,高中获校际西洋拳冠军,大学组建"中国功夫队",后开"振藩国术馆",著《基本中国拳法》,创立截拳道,在全美传播中华武术。李小龙打破了之前功夫片的虚假,开创了华人进军好莱坞的先河,让西方人开始认识和学习中国功

夫。成龙说:"没有李小龙,就没有我。"李连杰说:"李小龙是我的榜样。"

文化剪影 Cultural Outline

Bruce Lee, alive and active, had a passion for wushu throughout his life and got teachings from various Kungfu masters, whose ideas such as Taiji, Wuji and Yin-Yang theory are the core theory of Jeet Kune Do and Taiji **Diagram**① is Jeet Kune Do's symbol. Later, he studied from Ip Man for Wing Chun Gung-fu, whose middle-line theory and free combat are integral parts of Jeet Kune Do. He learned from Chan Heung for Choy Lay Fut, the biggest Wushu school in Hong Kong, advocating actual combat. He mastered from the essence of the northern wushu Shao-Han-Sheng, whose chains of flying kicks were his symbolic movements, praised as the "Deadly Ballet" in the movie and television circles. He learned from Jhoon-Goo-Rhee, a Korean known as father of American Taekwondo, Ed Parker, father of American Karate and Gene Lebll, father of American Jujitsu. Ultimately, he **synthesized**② all the strong points, created Jeet Kone Do and became a Wushu master.

李小龙生性好动,一生酷爱武术,师承多端,其中的太极、无极、阴阳论观点成为截拳道的核心理论,太极图就是截拳道的标志图。后来,他拜叶问为师,习得咏春拳,其中的中线理论、自由搏击成为截拳道不可或缺的内容。他向陈享学得香港最大的武术门派蔡李佛拳，崇尚实战；向邵汉生习得北方拳术精华，其连环飞腿成为李小龙的标志性动作，影视界将其誉为"致命的芭蕾"。他与美国跆拳道之父韩国人李峻九、美国空手道之父埃德·帕克、美国柔术之父吉恩·勒比尔等相互切磋，终集大成，创立截拳道，成为一代武学宗师。

Bruce Lee had an **indissoluble**③ bond with the movie and television circles. At the age of ten, he starred *Little Cheung*, which won a favorable reception. In 1965, he became the first Chinese actor who signed with Hollywood and starred in *The Green Hornet* the next year. He had been on a roll since then, full of confidence. *The Big Boss* set the highest box-office record of three million Hong Kong dollars, *Fist of Fury* broke the Asian record, and *Enter the Dragon* had a shocking record in America, having defeated lots of Hollywood **blockbusters**④, from which the word "Kungfu Movie" came into being.

李小龙与影视界有不解之缘。十岁时，他主演《细路祥》，获得好评。1965年，他成为好莱坞第一位签约华人演员，次年便主演《青蜂侠》。此后佳片不断，春风得意。《唐山大兄》创下了当时三百万港元的最高票房纪录，《精武门》打破了亚洲票房纪录，《龙争虎斗》在美国票房惊人，击败了许多好莱坞大片，"功夫片"一词由此诞生。

As the founder of Jeet Kune Do, Bruce Lee pioneered and promoted a comprehensive fighting sport. As a movie master, he made the term of "Chinese Kung Fu" popular all over the world. Bruce Lee, however, was worth remembering more than his great success in the movie and television industry and outstanding achievements in the Wushu field. It was he who created a "Chinese Wushu Whirlwind" around the world and changed the foreigners' **stereotype**⑤ of the Chinese people. Alike, it was he who became an **idol**⑥ of the global Chinese. His lots of firsts have further **molded**⑦ him into a role of "Chinese Culture Communication Ambassador".

作为截拳道创始人,李小龙开创并推动了综合格斗运动。作为电影大师,李小龙让"中国功夫"一词风靡世界。然而,李小龙值得被铭记的不仅仅是影视行业的巨大成功和武术领域的杰出成就,还有他在全球刮起的一场"中华武术旋风",是他改变了外国人对中国人的刻板印象。同样,是他成为青年全球华人的偶像。李小龙的诸多"第一"还塑造了他"中华文化传播大使"的角色。

佳句点睛　Punchlines

1. I'm first of all a martial artist and then an actor.
我首先是个武术家,然后才是演员。

2. Take impossible as possible and infinite as finite.
以无法为有法,以无限为有限。

3. Grab a handful of water, and it must **submit**⑧, without any hesitation. Add the pressure and the water will slip away. The softest things are not afraid of any beating.

你要抓一把水,水必会屈服,毫不犹疑。你加上压力,水便溜走。最软的东西是不惧击的。

情景对话 Situational Dialogue

A: What is your impression of Bruce Lee?

B: He was a great Wushu master, creator of Jeet Kune Do.

A: Do you know about his Jeet Kune Do?

B: The symbol of Jeet Kune Do consists of the "Taiji Diagram". In addition, Jeet Kune Do should also contain the median theory, the core theoretical foundation of Wing Chun Gung-fu.

A: What you said makes sense. Bruce Lee's success was based on the coasts of the Pacific Ocean that there were many foreign Wushu elements **assimilated**[⑨] into Jeet Kune Do.

B: I also know he often exchanged Wushu with some famous foreign Kungfu masters.

A: Rome is not built in one day. Besides his willingness to learn from various sources, his persistence was another reason for his great fame. For example, his learning of Taijiquan had lasted over twenty years within his short life. As far as the twenty-six elements of Jeet Kune Do are concerned, how long should he sacrifice to combine them together? Statistics show that his movie and TV works were more than fifteen and related programs are countless. It is another great wonder.

B: It's truly extraordinary and amazing.

A: 你对李小龙有什么印象?

B: 他是一代武学大师,截拳道创始人。

A: 你知道他的截拳道吗?

B: 截拳道的标志是由"太极图"构成的。此外,截拳道还包含咏春拳最核心的理论基础——中线理论。

A: 你说的有道理。李小龙的成功基于太平洋两岸,他将许多外来武术元素吸收进了截拳道。

B: 我知道,他经常和一些外国武术名师相互切磋。

A: 冰冻三尺,非一日之寒。除了愿意师从多端,坚持不懈也是李小龙盛誉有加的又一原因。比如,在其短暂的人生中,他学习太极拳就持续了二十多年。就截拳道的二十六个元素而言,他得花费多长时间才能将它们融合一起?统计显示其影视作品不止十五部,相关节目更是数不胜数。这是又一大奇迹。

B: 的确不同凡响,令人叹为观止。

生词注解　Notes

① diagram /ˈdaɪəɡræm/　*n.* 图解;示意图

② synthesize /ˈsɪnθəsaɪz/　*vt.* 综合;(通过化学手段或生物过程)合成

③ indissoluble /ˌɪndɪˈsɒljəbl/　*adj.* 牢不可破的;稳定持久的

④ blockbuster /ˈblɒkbʌstə(r)/　*n.* 轰动一时的电影;一度热卖的畅销书

⑤ stereotype /ˈsteriətaɪp/　*n.* 刻板印象;模式化观念(或形象)

杰出人物

⑥ idol /ˈaɪdl/　n. 偶像；神像

⑦ mold /məʊld/　vt. 塑造；浇铸

⑦ submit /səbˈmɪt/　vi. 屈服；提交

⑧ assimilate /əˈsɪməleɪt/　vt. 同化；吸收

第七部分 体坛名人

Part VII Sports Celebrities

姚明

Yao Ming

  导入语 Lead-in

　　姚明(1980～)，别名"小巨人""移动长城"。祖籍江苏苏州，生于上海。现任中国篮球协会主席，亚洲篮联主席。生于篮球世家，自幼爱读书，十八岁入国家队，开始职业篮球生涯。二十二岁入美国职业篮坛，九年征战，风靡世界。三十一岁退役，积极投身篮球事业，并致力于体育公益活动，荣获"中国篮球杰出贡献奖"。2016年，姚明入选NBA名人堂，成为中国第一人。他曾获得2002年"感动中国"年度人物奖，颁奖词这样写道："他用高超的体育技能，在一个强手如林的国家运动项目中占有了一席之地，成就了很多人的梦想，更成为中国人的骄傲。他出色的表现和随时听从祖国召唤的爱国精神，使他带给人们的思考已经远远超过了体育本身。"

文化剪影 Cultural Outline

During his four years of national professional basketball, Yao Ming was selected into the national all-star team in the first year, won the Asian Men's Basketball Championship next year, the Most Valuable Player (MVP) in the regular season of CBA in the third year and the finals' champion and MVP in the fourth year. During the nine years of playing basketball in the United States, he was selected for the all-star **lineup**[①] of NBA eight times and he set two team records for a 100% hit rate. After retirement, he acted as the image ambassador for Beijing's Olympic Bid, rated as one of the World's 50 Outstanding Leaders.

姚明征战国家职业篮球的四年间，首年入选国家明星队，次年获得亚洲男篮锦标赛冠军，第三年获得中国篮协常规赛"最有价值球员"，第四年夺得总冠军并获总决赛"最有价值球员"。九年征战美国期间，八次入选美国职业篮球全明星阵容，曾以100%命中率两次创造球队历史记录。退役后，他成为北京申奥形象大使，被评为"全球五十位杰出领袖人物"。

Yao Ming is the pride of the Chinese sports and the Chinese people. As a Chinese sportsman, though there was only four years since he set foot in the league, he made brilliant achievements, not only taking such titles as Asian championship and Chinese championship into pocket but also wearing the laurels of MVP; he realized the dream many people have been seeking for many years and has become a model of the athletes. As an international athlete, there was only eight years since he entered the basketball forum of the USA, but he made remarkable contributions, not only winning a place in the Kingdom of Basketball for his superb basketball skills but also advancing the internationalization of American professional basketball for his **harmonious**[②] exchanges; he has become a model of world sports.

姚明是中国体育的骄傲，也是中国人的骄傲。作为中国运动员，踏入联赛仅四年，他便成绩斐然，不仅把亚洲冠军、中国冠军收入囊中，也把最有价值球员的桂冠戴在头上，实现了很多人多年追求的梦想，成为体育健儿的榜样。作为国际球员，踏入美国篮坛仅八年，他便贡献卓越，不仅因高超的篮球技艺在"篮球王国"赢得一席之地，而且因和谐交流而推动了美国职业篮球的国际化，成为世界体育的榜样。

Yao Ming is also a model for the Chinese people. Training hard and striving **tenaciously**[③], he entered the NBA league as "Top Pick". He, **indomitable**[④] and **conscientious**[⑤], entered the American Memorial Basketball Hall of Fame. He, loving homeland and obeying her call, led Chinese basketball players to take part in many times of global competitions. Throwing himself into programs for public good, he founded Yao Fund and made many times of donations. Because of Yao Ming, Chinese basketball has been a cultural card of China. Yao Ming's influence has gone far beyond the realm of sports.

姚明也是中国人的榜样。他刻苦训练,顽强拼搏,以"状元秀"身份踏入美国职业篮球联赛。他不屈不挠,尽职尽责,入选美国篮球名人堂。他热爱祖国,听从召唤,多次带领中国球员参加世界性大赛。他投身公益,成立姚基金,并多次捐款。因为姚明,中国篮球成为中国的一张文化名片。姚明的影响已经远远超出了体育的范畴。

佳句点睛　Punchlines

1. If he doesn't pick me, I'm going to be his worst enemy.
如果他不选我,我就会成为最让他头痛的敌人。

2. Money is not why I came to the NBA. For me, the first year's salary is enough to last my lifetime.
我来NBA的目的不是赚钱,对于我来说,头一年的薪水就够我花一辈子了。

3. At present they're really stronger than me, but I believe I'll beat them in the near future.
现在他们确实比我强,但我相信在不久的将来我会打败他们。

情景对话 Situational Dialogue

A: Do you know how many kinds of Olympic Games there are?

B: There're three in total. They are the Olympics, the **Paralympic**⑥ Games and the Youth Olympics.

A: Have you heard of the Special Olympics?

B: Sorry, I forgot. It was founded by Eunice Kennedy Shriver, John Kennedy's younger sister.

A: In fact, Yao Ming pays special attention to the Special Olympics.

B: You mean Big Yao? He should be more interested in the Summer Olympics.

A: But people admire Yao Ming not just because "he's a true global basketball **icon**⑦."

B: What do you mean?

A: I mean, knowing Yao Ming aside from basketball will definitely benefit us more. As far as I know, while he was an athlete, Yao Ming initiated a charity run in Beijing and returned to his hometown from America specially to take part in the opening ceremony of Shanghai Special Olympics.

B: The **benevolent**⑧ love others. Without benevolence, who'd go back and forth for the **retarded**⑨ like that?

A: 你知道有多少种奥运会吗?

B: 共有三种。它们是奥运会、残奥会和青奥会。

A: 你听说过特奥会吗?

B: 不好意思,我忘了。它是约翰·肯尼迪的妹妹尤妮斯·肯尼迪·施莱佛创立的。

A: 事实上,姚明特别关注特奥会。

B: 你是说大姚?他应该对夏季奥运会更有兴趣才对。

A: 人们钦佩姚明可不仅仅是因为"他是一位真正的全球性篮球偶像"。

B: 此话怎讲?

A: 我是说,抛开篮球了解姚明,会让我们获益更多。据我所知,姚明担任运动员期间,就在北京发起慈善义赛,并特意从美国回到故乡,参加上海特奥会开幕式。

B: 仁者爱人。没有仁爱之心,谁会那样为智障人士来回奔波呢?

生词注解　Notes

① lineup /ˈlaɪnˌʌp/　n. 阵容;阵列

② harmonious /hɑːˈməʊnɪəs/　adj. 和睦的;和谐的

③ tenaciously /təˈneɪʃəslɪ/　adv. 顽强地;执着地

④ indomitable /ɪnˈdɒmɪtəbl/　adj. 不屈不挠的;毫不气馁的

⑤ conscientious /ˌkɒnʃɪˈenʃəs/　adj. 尽职尽责的;一丝不苟的

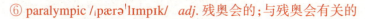

⑥ paralympic /ˌpærəˈlɪmpɪk/ adj. 残奥会的；与残奥会有关的
⑦ icon /ˈaɪkɒn/ n. 崇拜对象；图标
⑧ benevolent /bəˈnevələnt/ adj. 乐善好施的；慈善的
⑨ retarded /rɪˈtɑːdɪd/ adj. 弱智的；智力发育迟缓的

杰出人物

李娜

Li Na

导入语 Lead-in

李娜(1982~),祖籍湖北孝感,生于湖北武汉。中国网球杰出贡献者,亚洲首位网球大满贯女子单打冠军。7岁开始学网球,14岁入选省队,17岁入选国家队,4年后退役就读于华中科技大学。22岁重回赛场,再启夺冠之旅。27岁单飞,巡游世界,几经沉浮,终于惊艳法网,圆梦澳网,成为亚洲突破性网球选手,直到32岁退役,其世界排名第2长达25周,世界排名前10长达205周,位列亚洲第一。39岁入选"国际网球名人堂"。

文化剪影　Cultural Outline

Li Na entered the tennis world at the age of seven and has been inseparable ever since. She joined the provincial team at the age of fourteen, but her father died early and she supported her family at the age of sixteen. She was able to endure hardships and not complain of sufferings. She was willing to persevere and refuse to lose. At the age of seventeen she mainly focused on singles; struggling on the court resulted in her **forthright**① and sincere and **pragmatic**② style. During the fifteen-year career, she reached the finals of the Women's Tennis Association (WTA) Tour twenty-one times and won nine titles in this event and nineteen titles at the International Tennis Federation (ITF) Challenge, ranking second in the world for twenty-five weeks. In addition, she was many times rated as the "Best Female Athlete of China", released on the Forbes China Celebrity List. At the age of thirty-nine, she was selected into the "International Tennis Hall of Fame".

李娜7岁踏入网球世界，从此便与网球结下不解之缘。14岁进入省队，父亲的早逝和16岁起的养家经历，让李娜养成了能吃苦、不叫苦、愿坚持和不服输的性格。李娜17岁主攻单打，赛场征战造就了直率、真诚、务实的作风。15年职业生涯，她21次打入世界女子网协巡回赛决赛，共获得该项赛事9个冠军和19个国际网联挑战赛冠军，世界排名第2长达25周。此外，李娜多次被评为中国"中国最佳女运动员",登上福布斯中国名人榜,39岁时入选"国际网球名人堂"。

Li Na's tennis career was filled with historic breakthroughs. In her early career, together with Li Ting her partner, she took the women's doubles title at the WTA Tour, the first for Chinese players. After returning, she won the title at the Guangzhou International Women Singles Open and became the first singles title of China at the WTA tour; later she broke into the Wimbledon Champions, US Open and Australian Open, all creating the best Chinese records, ranking the first in China for two years on end; furthermore, she made the best Olympic record. In 2014, she became the first Asian and the oldest female singles champion of the **Centennial**③ Australian Open.

李娜的网球生涯充满了历史性突破。职业生涯早期,她和搭档李婷夺得世界女子网协巡回赛女双冠军,这是中国选手首次夺冠。复出后,她又夺得广州国际女子公开赛冠军,成为WTA巡回赛的首位中国女冠军。随后她闯入温网、美网和澳网,均创中国最佳记录,连续两年位列中国第一,再后创奥运会最佳记录。2014年,李娜成为百年澳网第一位亚洲人和最年长的女单冠军。

Li Na is a leading figure of Chinese tennis. As a tennis player with constant historic breakthrough, Li Na revealed superb **tactics**④, exquisite skills, a firm will and excellent sportsmanship.

李娜是中国网球的领军人物。作为不断有历史性突破的网球选手,李娜表现出高超的战术、精湛的技艺、坚定的意志和优秀的体育风尚。

佳句点睛　Punchlines

1. Representing China on the tennis court is my **supreme**⑤ honor.
在网球赛场上代表中国,是我至高无上的荣誉。

2. As long as you're alive, you're growing every moment in your life.
人这一辈子,每时每刻,只要活着,都在成长。

3. When you laugh, everyone will laugh with you. When you cry, you will cry alone.
当你笑的时候,所有人都陪你笑。当你哭的时候,只有你一个人哭。

情景对话　Situational Dialogue

A: What do you think of Li Na, Top Gun of Chinese Tennis?

B: Her legendary career shows that she is simply a myth.

A: She said, "I hope I can attract more attention to the tennis sport of China and even the whole Asia, which will be my career of life."

B: She is indeed creating a myth. Tennis is becoming more and more popular among Asians, especially in China. Perhaps you have noticed one detail: when Li Na won the "Memorial Cup", she was the oldest singles champion of the Centennial Australian Open. Studies show that the golden age for female tennis players is around twenty-six years old. But you know, Li Na started her solo performance at the age of twenty-seven.

A: She missed her **heyday**⑥ in sports. Indeed, her later accomplishments can be seen as challenging physiological limits.

B: Great. That's why I said she's a myth.

A: Right. Sister Na is well-deserved.

B: She is a vivid **illustration**⑦ of "Nothing Is Impossible". That's exactly what she said, "After all, this is between You and God, not between you and anyone else."

A: She also said, "My state is always ups and downs, and I have been walking between defeats and victories. I have slowly grasped this rule, so faced with failures, I'm getting more and more **rational**⑧."

B: So when she finally scaled the summit of her career, she could say proudly, "I'm very glad I can share this special joy and experience with my motherland, my team, my husband and my fans."

A: 你对"中国网球一姐"李娜有什么看法？

B: 她的传奇生涯表明，她简直就是一个神话。

A: 她说过:"我希望能够吸引更多的关注到中国甚至全亚洲的网球运动中,这将是我一生的事业。"

B: 她的确在创造神话。网球越来越受亚洲人的欢迎,尤其是在中国。或许你注意过一个细节,就是当李娜捧得"纪念杯"时,她已成为百年澳网最年长的单打冠军。研究表明,女网球手的黄金年华是26岁左右。可是,你知道,李娜单飞始于27岁。

A: 她错过了运动的鼎盛时期。事实上,她后来的成就可以被视为挑战生理极限。

B: 了不起,这就是我刚才说她是神话的原因。

A: 对,娜姐可谓实至名归。

B: 她就是"一切皆有可能"的生动诠释。正应了她那句话:"说到底,这是你和神之间的事,而绝不是你和他人之间的事。"

A: 她也说过:"我的状态总是起起落落,一直在失败和胜利间游走。我慢慢把握到了这种规律,面对失败,我开始变得更加理性。"

B: 所以,当她终于登上事业的巅峰时,才能自豪地说:"我很高兴我能够把这份特殊的喜悦和经历与我的祖国、我的团队、我的丈夫及我的球迷共同分享。"

生词注解 Notes

① forthright /ˈfɔːθraɪt/ *adj.* 直率的;坦诚的

② pragmatic /præɡˈmætɪk/ *adj.* 务实的;讲求实效的

③ centennial /senˈtenɪəl/ *adj.* 一百周年的

④ tactic /ˈtæktɪk/ *n.* 战术;招数

⑤ supreme /suːˈpriːm/ *adj.* 至高无上的；(程度)最大的

⑥ heyday /ˈheɪdeɪ/ *n.* 全盛时期；鼎盛时期

⑦ illustration /ˌɪləˈstreɪʃn/ *n.* 诠释；(说明事实的)故事

⑧ rational /ˈræʃnəl/ *adj.* 理性的；清醒的